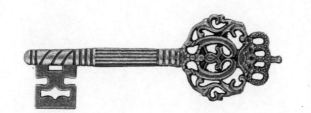

THE **KEY** TO ANSWERED **PRAYER**

RABBI KIRT A. SCHNEIDER

CHARISMA HOUSE

Visit the author's website at https://discoveringthejewishjesus.com.

Cataloging-in-Publication Data is on file with the Library of Congress.
International Standard Book Number: 978-1-63641-073-9
E-book ISBN: 978-1-63641-074-6

22 23 24 25 26 — 9 8 7 6 5 4 3 2 1
Printed in the United States of America

CONTENTS

PART I
The Patriarchs: From Wrestling to Blessing

PART II
Kings and Prophets: The Bold and the Wise

ACKNOWLEDGMENTS

WOULD LIKE TO express a special thanks to my editor at Charisma Media, Adrienne Gaines, who played such a crucial role in bringing this book to fruition. Without her help, this book would not have been published.

I would also like to acknowledge and thank two Discovering the Jewish Jesus consultants who have played key roles in my ministry, Steve Howard and Peter Clark.

"For from Him and through Him and to Him are all
things. To Him be the glory forever. Amen."
—ROMANS 11:36

Introduction

PARADISE LOST

I N THE BEGINNING there was no need for answered prayer. What an amazing thing to consider! The Book of Genesis—B'resheet, or "beginnings," in Hebrew—tells us God created male and female, giving them every seed-bearing plant, tree, and fruit to be their food. Adam was placed in the Garden of Eden to cultivate it, and Eve was created as a helper suitable for him. God walked with Adam and Eve in the garden, and they had no hunger, no sorrow, and no disease. It was a paradise on earth.

This was the relationship God first established with humanity, one of unhindered communication and companionship. We needed nothing other than Him. He was our Father, friend, and provider.

Many, priding themselves on our scientific and technological advancements, would say we've come a long way since the first man and woman walked the earth. Adam and Eve wouldn't recognize the world we now live in, with our cars, computers, and cell phones. Are we any better off, though? Obesity is epidemic in our nation, even as starvation rages in areas around the globe. We have devices able to connect us at lightning speed, but loneliness and feelings of intense isolation are on the rise. Our medical knowledge, though greater than ever before, is still put to the test by challenges such as COVID-19. Despite all our human understanding, we live on a planet full of hunger, sorrow, and disease, which were absent in the beginning.

Where is the God of the Bible in the midst of all this loneliness and pain? Why do our prayers often seem to go unanswered? As we hear of mass shootings in the news and of cancer rates across the land, it can seem as though God has turned away and left our messy world behind.

Searching for Something More

This sense of separation is real. As a boy, I had no idea I could connect personally with God. I lived in a large Jewish community in a suburb of Cleveland, Ohio, where I attended synagogue, memorized prayers, and learned our Jewish religious traditions. I went to Hebrew school three days a week in preparation of my Bar Mitzvah at age thirteen, but my hunger for God was still not satisfied, and I was left feeling spiritually empty. In my late teens I was so intrigued by a yogi from India's claims of supernatural feats that I bought a copy of his autobiography, convinced there must be something more to this life than chasing after money and recognition.

People all around the world are searching for something more. Where does this deep longing come from? Why do so many of us feel isolated and alone?

Our sense of separation goes all the way back to the Garden of Eden. In Genesis 2:16–17, before Eve was even created, "the LORD God commanded the man, saying, 'From any tree of the garden you may eat freely; but from the tree of the knowledge of good and evil you shall not eat, for in the day that you eat from it you will surely die.'"

When the serpent later offered Eve the fruit, he (the devil) scoffed at God's warning. "You surely will not die!" the serpent told her. "For God knows that in the day you eat from it your eyes will be opened, and you will be like God, knowing good and evil" (Gen. 3:4–5).

Yes, Eve was deceived, but Adam knowingly disobeyed God's direct orders to him. Together he and his wife ate of the forbidden fruit. Thus armed with the knowledge of good and evil, they might have thought they had all the answers they needed—but that's not the way it played out. Because of their rebellion, sin entered the world, and separation from God was the result.

"Therefore the LORD God sent him out from the garden of Eden....So He drove the man out; and at the east of the garden of Eden He stationed the cherubim and the flaming sword which turned every direction to guard the way to the tree of life" (Gen. 3:23–24).

Twice this passage describes man being sent out. Sin cut us off from the presence of the holy God. Spiritual and physical death became earthly realities, and we now live in a paradise lost.

How does all this relate to the subject of prayer?

While there was no hunger, sorrow, or disease in the Garden of Eden, we cannot escape such issues in our modern world. Many of us go to work each day just to put food on the table and cover another week's worth of bills. Each of us wrestles with tough questions and private grief. We all know friends or family members struggling with serious medical issues. In the midst of this, prayer often becomes a last resort. Instead of first reaching for God out of intimacy with Him, we often complain to Him at the end of a situation and blame Him for its outcome. Our faith wavers. If we continue praying at all, we might do so simply to impress others or to make them feel better, relying on empty words that never really align with the heart of God.

Knowing God's heart is key. He knows each of us intimately, having formed us in our mothers' wombs (Ps. 139:13), and He wants us to know Him too. He proved this to me one summer night in 1978 in my home in Pepper Pike, Ohio. With my eyes still closed, I was awakened from sleep and experienced a vision of Jesus Christ on the cross. A beam of red light shot down from the skies above, washing over Jesus' head. Though I'd received no Christian witness in my life, I understood for the first time that Jesus is the way to God.

I bought a copy of the New Testament soon afterward and threw away the yogi's autobiography. At twenty years old I started my journey out of darkness into the light.

Our Deepest Need

We all have an opportunity for a relationship with God. Though it was lost in the Garden of Eden, it was restored fully when Jesus paid the penalty for our sins upon the cross. He bridged the separation between God and humanity. Matthew 27:51 says that at the moment of Jesus' death outside Jerusalem, "the veil of the temple was torn in two from top to bottom." God tore away the barrier and now allows us to draw near to Him with confidence through Jesus' blood. (See Hebrews 4:16.) We do not have to hide in shame. We are now able to talk with Him and know His will.

This is a crucial part of the gospel, the good news. Without it we would have no chance of moving God's heart, and there would be no reason to write a book about praying in such a way that our prayers are answered. We would live only for ourselves, feeding our bellies, working for earthly treasures, and trusting our diets and exercise regimens to fend off sickness. Many people do exactly that.

Instead, through the sacrifice of Jesus we have been reunited with our Father, sons and daughters of the living God, heirs of His riches and grace. Our deepest need has always been relationship, and we were created for companionship with God. In Him we live and move and have our being. He wants us to come boldly into His presence. There's no need to be shy or afraid. "This is the confidence which we have before Him," declares 1 John 5:14, "that, if we ask anything according to His will, He hears us."

That is an incredible promise! But how can we know His will?

In the coming chapters we will study the prayers of patriarchs, kings, prophets, the apostles, and even Jesus to see why their prayers moved God's heart and caused Him to respond. You'll even learn about a regular person, a "nobody," whose short prayer has become known all around the world. God loves working through little people to do big things, which is especially encouraging to me since I stand barely five feet seven in my shoes.

As we study the prayers of these individuals who walked closely with God and see how God answered them, we will learn how to pray in a way that moves God to act on our behalf. You see, when we pray according to Scripture, we can have great confidence and expectation that God will answer, because we're asking God for the things He desires for us.

No matter what circumstances life throws your way, there is

power to be found in talking with God. Are you ready, beloved ones, to study His Word with me? Let's throw open the doors to a deeper relationship and to prayers that resonate with God.

PART I

The Patriarchs: From Wrestling to Blessing

Chapter 1

A PRAYER FOR PROTECTION, PROVISION, AND DELIVERANCE

> Then Jacob made a vow, saying, "If God will be with me
> and will keep me on this journey that I take, and will give
> me food to eat and garments to wear, and I return to my
> father's house in safety, then the LORD will be my God."
> —GENESIS 28:20–21

IN GENESIS 28, Jacob was running for his life after robbing his twin brother, Esau, of their father's blessing. You may know the story. The name Jacob—Ya'akov in Hebrew—means trickster or supplanter, and it was a name he lived up to. Jacob came out of the womb clinging to his older brother's heel. Then, years later, when Esau came to him famished after a hunting trip, Jacob agreed to feed him on one condition: that Esau would sell him his birthright. Esau did just that, trading his birthright for some bread and lentil stew.

That was bad, but it only got worse. When the time came for Jacob and Esau's father, Isaac, to bless his firstborn son, Jacob conspired with his mother, Rebekah, to steal the blessing that belonged to Esau. While Esau was still hunting for the game to make the stew his father requested, Jacob was at Isaac's bedside, serving him a meal Rebekah had prepared. He even went so far as to wear Esau's clothes and put animal skin on his hands and neck to fool Isaac into thinking he was with his hairier son. Just like that, Jacob stole Esau's blessing.

As a result, Jacob found himself running from his brother, who wanted to kill him. In the midst of his running, Jacob was in the wilderness sleeping on a rock when he had a dramatic dream.

> Behold, a ladder was set on the earth with its top reaching to heaven; and behold, the angels of God were ascending and descending on it. And behold, the LORD stood above it and said, "I am the LORD, the God of your father Abraham and the God of Isaac; the land on which you lie, I will give it to you and to your descendants. Your descendants will also be like the dust of the earth, and you will spread out to the west and to the east and to the north and to the south; and in you and in your descendants shall all the families of the earth be blessed. Behold, I am with you and will keep you wherever you go, and will bring you back to this land; for I will not leave you until I have done what I have promised you."
>
> —GENESIS 28:12–15

Jacob's dream marked a significant turning point in his life. There in the wilderness, God revealed Himself to him. He was no longer just the God of Abraham and Isaac. Now He was promising to also make Jacob into a great nation, to give him the land on which he lay and make his descendants like the dust of the earth.

When he woke up, Jacob knew something profound had happened to him, and he said, "How awesome is this place! This is none other than the house of God, and this is the gate of heaven" (Gen. 28:17). Jacob named the place Bethel, which in Hebrew means house of God. Then he made the vow quoted in part at the beginning of this chapter: "If God will be with me and will keep me on this journey that I take, and will give me food to eat and garments to wear, and I return to my father's house in safety, then the LORD will be my God. This stone, which I have set up as a pillar, will be God's house, and of all that You give me I will surely give a tenth to You" (Gen. 28:20–22).

God, Protect Me!

In this simple prayer, Jacob was sharing his deepest needs with his Father—*to feel protected and secure.* When Jacob prayed, "If God will be with me and will keep me on this journey that I take...," he was looking for assurance that God would not leave him. He was saying in essence, "God, I need You. Please don't leave me alone. Guard me on this journey." Beloved, when you ask God to keep you, He hears you. In fact, when God made you in His own image, He put a need for Him in your heart, and He wants you to depend on Him to keep you safe.

Psalm 27 says, "The LORD is my light and my salvation; whom shall I fear? The LORD is the defense of my life; whom shall I dread? When evildoers came upon me to devour my flesh, my adversaries and my enemies, they stumbled and fell. Though a host encamp against me, my heart will not fear; though war arise against me, in spite of this I shall be confident....For in the day of trouble He will conceal me in His tabernacle; in the secret place of His tent He will hide me; He will lift me up on a rock" (vv. 1–3, 5). When we were newborn infants in the world, we thought everything was going to be OK. I realize some people grew up in difficult situations and didn't feel safe at home, but in general God makes children feel safe. When people grow up in a healthy environment, they feel nurtured and protected by boundaries and family structure. This is the way God intended it.

As a young person in Cleveland, I felt secure. I trusted that my dad and mom had all the answers, and I was unaware of all the dangers lurking outside our home. Only as I got older did I understand that murders and kidnappings were happening and that people were getting into car accidents on the road.

As we get older and realize this world is a dangerous place, God wants us to turn to Him to feel safe. David wrote, "Surely I have composed and quieted my soul; like a weaned child rests against his mother, my soul is like a weaned child within me" (Ps. 131:2). David had come to feel so safe and secure through his relationship with God that it reminded him of the safety he felt as a little child being held by his mother.

This is what the Father desires for us as His children. He wants us to know we can depend on Him to keep us. In Him we can abide. Even though we walk through the valley of the shadow of death, we need fear no evil (Ps. 23:4).

God, Provide for Me!

Jacob didn't stop at praying for protection; he pressed further, asking God to give him "food to eat and garments to wear." He prayed for provision, that the Lord would put a roof over his head and food in his stomach.

God wants us to have confidence that no matter where we go on this journey we call life or what stage of life we're in—whether we're ten years old, young adults, middle-aged, or elderly—we can depend on Him to be with us, keep us, and provide for us.

Beloved, don't take this for granted. Believe this promise from your Father. Confess that Father is keeping and providing for you and will continue to do so. Declare that you don't have to fear the future because even when you're old, God is going to keep you, provide for you, and bring you everything you need to lead an abundant life in Him.

In addition to your confession, ask Father God to keep you safe and provide everything you need. When you go outside your front door and get into your car, ask God to protect you as you're driving, to give His angels charge over you lest you dash your foot against a stone. Ask Him to "supply all your needs according to His riches in glory in Christ Jesus" (Phil. 4:19). When you ask God to keep you and provide for you, He will be faithful to do those very things because your Father is concerned about your needs.

Perhaps like Jacob you need to feel secure and safe. Perhaps you're feeling vulnerable or threatened by life. Maybe you're fighting fears of sickness or of running out of money. I want you to know that God loves you, and just as He answered Jacob's prayer, He will answer your prayer as you cling to and depend on Him. God is going to bring you to the end of your journey safely, and He will provide everything you need along the way because He is the God of lights and every good and perfect gift comes from Him.

Perhaps you are irritated by all this talk of needing God and relying on Him. You feel pride rising up in you, a sense that you can handle it all on your own. You like to believe you are an independent person, in need of nobody. Could this attitude be keeping you from experiencing an intimate and trusting relationship with your Creator? Please hear me: the spirit of pride and independence is demonic. You have an opportunity to break Satan's hold by getting down on your knees this very moment and asking Father God, in the name of the Lord Jesus, to forgive you and cleanse you of pride. Ask Him to come into your life and develop a love relationship with you. It is perhaps the most critical decision you will ever make.

Jesus said if God knows how to take care of the sparrows that are here today and gone tomorrow, if He clothes the lilies of the field in a grander fashion than King Solomon, how much more will He take care of His own children? (See Matthew 6:25–34.) Father is going to provide. Not a sparrow falls to the ground without Him knowing it. He knows what you'll need even before you become aware of it. You are safe in His arms, and you can have confidence that when you pray for His provision and protection, He will answer.

God, Deliver Me!

Fast-forward twenty years. Jacob is married to Leah and Rachel and has eleven strong sons. After spending two decades working for his father-in-law, Jacob had acquired vast livestock and was "exceedingly prosperous" (Gen. 30:43). It was just as God promised him at Bethel.

Yet Jacob had a problem. God told him it was time to return to his homeland, Canaan, because that's where God would bless him. But that's also where Esau lived, and the last time Jacob was near his brother, Esau was plotting to kill him. Jacob needed God, and he knew it. So he poured his heart out to the Lord.

> O God of my father Abraham and God of my father Isaac, O Lord, who said to me, "Return to your country and to your relatives, and I will prosper you," I am unworthy of all the lovingkindness and of all the faithfulness which You have shown to Your servant; for with my staff only I crossed this Jordan, and now I have become two companies. Deliver me, I pray, from the hand of my brother, from the hand of Esau; for I fear him, that he will come and attack me and the mothers with the children. For You said, "I will surely prosper you and make your descendants as the sand of the sea, which is too great to be numbered."
>
> —Genesis 32:9–12

When Jacob left his father's house, he had nothing. But God blessed and multiplied him, and he became rich in the Lord. In his prayer Jacob remembered how far God had brought him and all that He had done for him, but he again needed reassurance because he was afraid Esau was going to attack him.

So he went to God in prayer and told Him all about his fear. He held nothing back. That is such a beautiful thing. Jacob had the type of relationship with God that allowed him to talk to God about his fear just as he would talk with a friend. He knew God as an intimate companion, as someone who loved him, as someone upon whom he could cast his burden.

In the Gospel of John we read that John, the disciple whom

Jesus loved, leaned his head on Jesus' bosom at the Last Supper. Just think about how safe John must have felt in his relationship with Jesus to lean his head on Yeshua's bosom. In the same way, God wants you to know that He loves you. He wants you to be just as intimate with Him as Jacob was in the Book of Genesis and as John was at the Last Supper, which was actually a Passover meal. You can share your heart with God. You can tell Him when you're afraid. You can talk to Him about your worries and fears and know that He's going to watch over you, that His goodness goes with you, that He's a shield of protection around you, and that He's going to keep you safe until the end of your life.

After he told the Father he was afraid, Jacob prayed, "Lord, deliver me from Esau." Perhaps you can relate to Jacob. Maybe you need deliverance from something in your life. I want you to know that Jesus is a deliverer. The God who broke in to deliver the children of Israel out of Egypt is still working miracles today. He is still setting captives free. I can think of many times when Father delivered me. He saved me from going to dangerous places, from making decisions that would have been disastrous, and from demonic attack, which sometimes manifested through human beings. God is real, beloved, and He doesn't want you to know Him just as the God who delivered Jacob. He wants you to know Him individually and personally as the God who will deliver you.

Maybe you're in debt or going through a health crisis. Maybe you're in the midst of a legal battle or facing turmoil at work. No matter what the situation is, you can ask God to be your deliverer. Just tell Him your need. Humble yourself before Him and confess to Him any sin you might have committed that put you in the situation. Then ask Him to forgive you and set you free. Be specific—tell Him exactly what you need deliverance from—then thank Him for the victory. He is the Lord our banner, Yahweh Nissi, the triumphant God who reigns in victory, and in Him you are more than a conqueror (Rom. 8:37).

For much of his life, Jacob was not a morally outstanding person. He was a trickster and a usurper, yet God still loved him. We are "saved…not on the basis of deeds which we have done in righteousness, but according to His mercy" (Titus 3:5). Even as God's mercy was on Jacob, so it is on us in Messiah Jesus. Even as God heard Jacob's prayers, He hears your prayers. You have the same Father Jacob had.

Chapter 2

A PLEA FOR GOD'S BLESSING

Then he said, "Let me go, for the dawn is breaking." But
he said, "I will not let you go unless you bless me."
—GENESIS 32:26

GOD WANTS TO bless you. Do you believe that? Do you believe God wants to prosper you? Some people have rejected this truth because of extremes in teaching on prosperity, but let's not throw the baby out with the bathwater. Jesus said, "I came that they may have life, and have it abundantly" (John 10:10). And John the apostle wrote, "Beloved, I pray that in all respects you may prosper and be in good health, just as your soul prospers" (3 John 1:2).

You don't have to be afraid or ashamed of asking God to bless and expand you. God wants to give you increase. He doesn't want you to just get by; He wants you to have enough to give to others. God wants you to walk in blessing. He wants you to be a sign and a wonder.

Healthy parents want to bless their children; they want to see them happy. God wants that even more. Jesus said, "If you then, being evil, know how to give good gifts to your children, how much more will your Father who is in heaven give what is good to those who ask Him!" (Matt. 7:11). Beloved, we can ask God to bless us. We can ask God to prosper us. We can be confident of this because of the window we have into Jacob's relationship with Father God through his prayer life.

As we saw in the previous chapter, God called Jacob to return to his country, which meant he would be forced to face his brother Esau for the first time after stealing his birthright. At this point in his story, Jacob has been told that Esau is coming to meet him, and Jacob doesn't know what he is about to encounter. Like so many of us, he hoped for the best but prepared for the worst. He selected from his flocks a gift for his brother: "two hundred female goats and twenty male goats, two hundred ewes and twenty rams, thirty milking camels and their colts, forty cows and ten bulls, twenty female donkeys and ten male donkeys" (Gen. 32:14–15).

He sent the present on ahead of him while he remained in their camp, and that night, Jacob had an encounter that would literally change his life.

> Then Jacob was left alone, and a man wrestled with him until daybreak. When he saw that he had not prevailed against him, he touched the socket of his thigh; so the socket of Jacob's thigh was dislocated while he wrestled with him. Then he said, "Let me go, for the dawn is breaking." But he said, "I will not let you go unless you bless me." So he said to him, "What is your name?" And he said, "Jacob." He said, "Your name shall no longer be Jacob, but Israel; for you have striven with God and with

men and have prevailed." Then Jacob asked him and said, "Please tell me your name." But he said, "Why is it that you ask my name?" And he blessed him there. So Jacob named the place Peniel, for he said, "I have seen God face to face, yet my life has been preserved."

—GENESIS 32:24–30

A Spirit of Desperation

Jacob needed God, and he knew it. He told the angel, "I'm not going to let go unless you bless me." He was desperate. And when Jacob walked away from this wrestling match with God, he walked away blessed. He walked away with a different confidence. He walked away with a new name and a different destiny. And later when he faced his brother, Jacob walked away with a new relationship with Esau. Instead of striking Jacob with a sword, Esau ran and embraced him. The foundation of all these blessings was Jacob's desperation.

Jesus said, "Blessed are those who hunger and thirst for righteousness, for they shall be satisfied" (Matt. 5:6). God will answer us when we're desperate. When we mean business with God, God will mean business with us. He will answer us according to our desperation. So beloved, how desperate are you?

This reminds me of a poem I once heard called "The Prayer of Cyrus Brown":

"The proper way for a man to pray,"
Said Deacon Lemuel Keyes,
"And the only proper attitude
Is down upon his knees."

"No, I should say the way to pray,"
Said Rev. Doctor Wise,

"Is standing straight with outstretched arms
And rapt and upturned eyes."

"Oh, no; no, no," said Elder Slow,
"Such posture is too proud:
A man should pray with eyes fast closed
And head contritely bowed."

"It seems to me his hands should be
Austerely clasped in front.
With both thumbs pointing toward the ground,"
Said Rev. Doctor Blunt.

"Las' year I fell in Hodgkin's well
Head first," said Cyrus Brown,
"With both my heels a-stickin' up,
My head a-pinting down;

"An' I made a prayer right then an' there—
Best prayer I ever said,
The prayingest prayer I ever prayed,
A-standing on my head."[1]

Jesus said, "From the days of John the Baptist until now the kingdom of heaven suffers violence, and violent men take it by force" (Matt. 11:12). This holy violence is a form of spiritual desperation. It's the type of heart that Jacob had when he said, "I'm not going to let go unless you bless me." We have to get to the place where we say, "Enough is enough. I'm tired of leading a lukewarm life. I'm tired of living in defeat. I declare that I must walk in victory."

It's time to let Father God know that you're desperate—that you will no longer settle for a life that's average. Declare, "I'm not going to let go unless You bless me and I live in victory. I want to live with Your power and blessing on my life! I must know You!"

God responds to a heart that's desperate. When you come to the end of yourself, that's when God really works. The apostle Paul wrote, "And He has said to me, 'My grace is sufficient for you, for power is perfected in weakness.' Most gladly, therefore, I will rather boast about my weaknesses, so that the power of Christ may dwell in me. Therefore I am well content with weaknesses, with insults, with distresses, with persecutions, with difficulties, for Christ's sake; for when I am weak, then I am strong" (2 Cor. 12:9–10). A new strength, anointing, and empowerment will come into your life if you'll do what Jacob did and come to God from a place of desperation.

Put a Demand on God

In addition to being desperate, Jacob had faith. He believed God would bless him. Again, Jacob said in Genesis 32:26, "I will not let you go unless you bless me." That took faith. Jacob didn't ask God to bless him, all the while doubting whether God was truly there or if He would respond to his request. No. Jacob believed God could and would bless him if he would demand it by faith.

Of course, God is the sovereign Lord, and He does what He wants, but we need to understand that in order to receive from God, we have to put a demand on Him. I'm not talking about thinking we can control God. I'm talking about knowing who God is and having enough faith in Him to say, "I believe this is who You are, I believe this is what You said, I believe I can have what You said I can have, and I'm not going to let go of You until I've received it." This takes faith. People who receive from God "believe that He is, and that He is a rewarder of those who diligently seek Him" (Heb. 11:6, NKJV). He will do what He said He will do.

Beloved, what do you think about God? Do you think God is distant? Do you think He is arbitrary? Do you think you can't count on Him? Are you unsure of what God will do, so you don't anticipate being blessed? Or do you have the type of faith that rises up in you and takes hold of God's Word? Jesus said, "If the Son makes you free, you will be free indeed" (John 8:36). Do you have the type of faith that says, "Jesus, I believe that in You I am free; I believe that through You I can walk in freedom; I believe that through You I can walk in victory"?

The Bible says we can reign in this life through Christ Jesus (Rom. 5:17). If you have faith that Jesus is who He said He is, if shame has been broken off your life because you know that you're accepted in Him through His blood, then you're going to rise up like Jacob did and say, "Lord, I'm taking hold of Your Word. I believe You meant what You said. I believe You are who You say You are. I believe I can have and walk in what Your Word says I can have. I take hold of You now. I refuse to let go. This is mine in Yeshua, and I declare that I walk in it in Jesus' name."

This is the type of faith that moves mountains. This is the type of faith that lays hold of what God's Word says the Father wants to release—but He releases it only through desperation and faith. Jesus said, "Blessed are the poor in spirit, for theirs is the kingdom of heaven" (Matt. 5:3). What does it mean to be poor in spirit? It means to recognize that we're empty without receiving Messiah Jesus' fullness. Jacob had faith that he could be blessed, and his example teaches us that God's desire is to bless us.

Sometimes we take our cues from the world around us. We see our parents who are Christians living at a low level of victory. Or we look at the people in our congregations and see them living at a low level of victory. Perhaps all around you are good, well-meaning believers in Yeshua whose lives are filled with worry, strife, and fear so you think that's as good as it gets. Could it be that you are settling for less because you've set your bar according to the people around you rather than according to God's Word? Paul said if we compare ourselves with others rather than with God's Word, we will lack understanding (2 Cor. 10:12). The Scripture says we've been blessed with every spiritual blessing in the heavenly places (Eph. 1:3), that God has not given us a spirit of fear but one of love and of power and a sound mind (2 Tim. 1:7), and that Jesus came to give life and give it more abundantly (John 10:10).

When you really believe God's Word and that you can have what He says you can have, you'll labor and contend for those things in prayer, and more and more you'll enter into the Father's fullness.

The Power of Pressing In

Again, Jacob said, "I'm not going to let go unless You bless me." But what is the blessing we are seeking? It is every spiritual blessing in the heavenly places. It is the fullness of love, joy, freedom, beauty, and power that comes from being set free to live in union and friendship with our Creator. This fullness doesn't come in a second; we enter into it more and more as we press in through prayer.

Just as the children of Israel drove the Amorites, Hittites, Jebusites, and Canaanites out of the Promised Land little by little (Exod. 23:30), so we drive out the enemies of God's promise to us little by little. Through prayer we rise up and drive out the darkness. We break the power of fear, lack, and worry, and as we do, we press in to eternal life. We press in to the Spirit. We press in to the kingdom of God, and we enter into more love, more *shalom*, more harmony, and more power.

As we press in, we enter into a greater fullness of what Yeshua purchased for us with His blood and we experience what Jacob prayed for: blessing. But we must be desperate for it, we must believe we can have it, and then we must contend for it in prayer. The apostle Paul said in Ephesians 6 that our fight is not against flesh and blood but against principalities and forces of spiritual wickedness in heavenly places. "He who overcomes will inherit these things [eternal life]" (Rev. 21:7).

Beloved, God wants to bless us, and we can be confident that He will bless us, because we are praying to the same God Jacob prayed to—a God who blesses His people. You don't have to be perfect. You just need to be hungry and press in. My friend, there is more for you. As you reach out to God in faith, you're going to enter more and more into the abundant life Jesus purchased for you.

After Jacob wrestled with the angel, God changed his name to Israel, and he became the father of the twelve tribes of the nation of Israel. According to Ephesians 2:12–13, as a believer in Yeshua, you have been added to the commonwealth of Israel. You are part of that same spiritual lineage, and not only has the blessing of Abraham come upon you (Gal. 3:14–29), but also you have received the same favor that was upon Jacob.

Chapter 3

A PRAYER TO SEE GOD'S GLORY

> Then Moses said to the LORD, "...Now therefore, I
> pray You, if I have found favor in Your sight, let me
> know Your ways....If Your presence does not go with
> us, do not lead us up from here. For how then can it
> be known that I have found favor in Your sight, I and
> Your people?...I pray You, show me Your glory!"
> —EXODUS 33:12–13, 15–16, 18

IN EXODUS 33 we find one of the most famous prayers in
Scripture uttered by one of the most famous men in Scripture. Moses was the great deliverer of Israel, the one God
raised up to lead His people out of slavery in Egypt and to the
edge of the Promised Land. If you ask Jewish people today who
the most outstanding person in the Hebrew Bible is—which
Jews call the Tanakh and Christians call the Old Testament—
most will tell you Moses.

Unlike other prophets, Moses didn't hear from God through
dreams and visions. The Bible says, "The LORD used to speak
to Moses face to face, just as a man speaks to his friend" (Exod.

33:11). Can you imagine? How incredible and intimate his relationship with God must have been for the Lord to call him His friend. Another amazing characteristic of Moses is that Scripture says he "was very humble, more than any man who was on the face of the earth" (Num. 12:3).

This is why Moses' prayer in Exodus 33 has so much to teach us. In this chapter God had called Moses to leave Sinai, promising to send an angel to go before the Israelites to drive out their enemies. But this was on the heels of the fiasco with the golden calf, when the Israelites chose to abandon God and worship an idol. God was so angry with His people that He wanted to destroy them. He relented only because Moses interceded on their behalf. So when God instructed Moses to leave Sinai, He said, "I will not go up in your midst, because you are an obstinate people, and I might destroy you on the way" (Exod. 33:3).

This is when Moses went to the Lord in prayer.

> Then Moses said to the LORD, "See, You say to me, 'Bring up this people!' But You Yourself have not let me know whom You will send with me. Moreover, You have said, 'I have known you by name, and you have also found favor in My sight.' Now therefore, I pray You, if I have found favor in Your sight, let me know Your ways that I may know You, so that I may find favor in Your sight. Consider too, that this nation is Your people."...Then he said to Him, "If Your presence does not go with us, do not lead us up from here. For how then can it be known that I have found favor in Your sight, I and Your people? Is it not by Your going with us, so that we, I and Your people, may be

distinguished from all the other people who are upon the face of the earth?"

...Then Moses said, "I pray You, show me Your glory!"

—Exodus 33:12–13, 15–16, 18

In this petition from a man who walked so closely with God, we see what was in Moses' heart, what he desired from the Lord, and what God wants to give us, His children, as well.

Know God's Love and Favor

In verse 12 Moses said to the Lord, "You have said, 'I have known you by name, and you have also found favor in My sight.'" Consider those words for a moment. They are as true for us as they were for Moses. God knows us, He loves us, and His favor is on us. Do you believe that? Do you believe God loves you and knows you by name and that His favor is on your life? Beloved, if we're going to move visible and invisible realms through prayer, we must be convinced of that.

In Psalm 139 David reveals that while we were yet in the womb, Father God knew us—that He saw our unformed substance. Jesus said the hairs on our heads are numbered (Luke 12:7). You can be sure that God knows and loves you, specifically, personally, and uniquely. He designed you just for Himself, and He has a definite destiny and plan for your life.

Moses was confident of that. He knew the Lord had called him by name and that God's favor was on him. God wants you to be convinced of the same thing. Some of us are trapped in a spirit of dread and gloom. We're afraid of what's going to happen tomorrow or down the road in the future. Why? Because we're not confident that God's favor is on our lives. We're not confident that goodness and mercy are going to follow us all the days of our lives (Ps. 23:6). We're not confident that God has a good plan for us. We're not confident that we exist in the protection of our Father's love.

Beloved, you and I need to believe that God knows us and that His favor is on us. If you have a hard time believing that, do what Moses did. He asked the Lord to help him become more convinced of that truth.

In verse 12 Moses said, "You have said, 'I have known you by name, and you have also found favor in My sight.'" Then, in verse 13 he said, "Now therefore, I pray You, if I have found favor in Your sight, let me know Your ways that I may know You, so that I may find favor in Your sight." It is clear in verse 12 that Moses knew God's favor was on him. But what we see in verse 13 is Moses asking for reassurance. He's saying, "Lord, help me realize this more."

There's nothing wrong with asking the Father for reassurance. Remember the man who prayed, "Lord, I believe. Help my unbelief!" (Mark 9:24, MEV)? Even now we can pray, "Father, help me to know in an even greater way the abundance of Your love and favor on my life. I receive now the confidence of Your favor on my life."

Beloved, I decree and declare over you as a father to the church (1 Cor. 4:15)—God knows you, He loves you, and His favor is on your life. Receive that truth. Receive the knowledge of His favor. Receive His love and *shalom*.

Humbly Rely on the Father

Moses goes on to say in verse 15, "If Your presence does not go with us, do not lead us up from here." This speaks of Moses' humility. Moses was not presumptuous. He said, "Father, if You don't go with me, if Your presence isn't going before me, let us not go." This, again, tells us how dependent on God Moses was. He was afraid of going out there and relying on his own strength. So many people are making decisions that result in failure and are taking actions that lead to unfruitfulness because they don't have the attitude Moses displayed when he said, "Father, if You don't go with us, if Your presence doesn't go with us, I'm not going to go."

For some of us, instead of walking in that type of humility, we're walking presumptuously. We're not relying on the Father. We're not afraid of relying on our own abilities. We just rush out there like a bull in a china stop, doing whatever we think is best, not realizing that unless Father God blesses us, we're putting ourselves in a dangerous place. In this prayer, Moses teaches us that we need to come to a place of humility and recognize that unless we're relying on God to go before us every day, we're positioning ourselves to fail. Even Jesus said, "Truly, truly, I say to you, the Son can do nothing of Himself, unless it is something He sees the Father doing; for whatever the Father does, these things the Son also does in like manner" (John 5:19).

We can't get in our cars and just assume we will be safe as we drive. We can't just assume things are going to go well for our families. We must rely on God's protection. We must go before Him in prayer daily, asking Him to keep us safe and guide us by His Spirit. Only when we put ourselves in a posture of reliance, as Moses did, can we be confident that the Lord is blessing our families, giving us wisdom, and leading us in the way we should go.

In Judaism, we call this *devekut*, which means cleaving to God. There was a point in my life approximately fifteen years ago when I ran into a crisis of faith. I had been observing for years that so many people around me who were naming the name of Jesus seemed to be living tragic lives of failure. It wasn't just that many were slipping here and there; it seemed as though their whole lives were marked by defeat. And it didn't line up for me with what the Bible said we should be walking in as believers—that we are victorious in Christ and that we reign in life through Messiah Yeshua. But with no clear answer, I just buried this disconnect between what the Bible said we should be walking in and what I was observing in the lives of so many people around me. But one day it surfaced, and I couldn't deny it any longer.

It was a cold January night, and I had brought my congregation's dance team with me to minister at a service where I was preaching. After the service, I was packing up my things, and the husband of one of the dancers ran into the church from the parking lot and said, "My wife just fell on the ice in the parking lot!" Now, his wife looked to be about sixty years old, and she was a very fragile woman, so I knew when she fell, her bones hit that asphalt parking lot hard.

At this point I just couldn't deny the disconnect between what God had said that we should be walking in and what I saw happening in the lives of so many who called themselves believers. And I said to God, "Lord, why didn't You prevent this from happening? This woman just got done dancing for You! I mean, surely You could have kept her from falling in that parking lot. I know Your ways are above my ways, but I just can't believe this was for a good purpose. Father, until I understand why I'm seeing these bad things happen in the lives of Your people, I'm not going to be able to move forward in my faith."

I wasn't walking away from the Lord; I was only saying that I wasn't going to go further until He gave me an answer. A few days later, as I was carrying this dilemma in my heart, I had a sense that God was going to answer me, but I was sad inside. Then, a few days after that, I was leaving an appointment, and as I was driving my vehicle out of the parking lot, the Holy Spirit clearly spoke to me. It wasn't audible, but I definitely heard the Spirit in my heart, and He said this to me: "The reason you're seeing My people falling and failing is because they're not trusting Me." But when He said the word *trusting*, it was filled with revelation. What He was actually communicating to me was the idea of clinging. He said the word *trust*, but what He meant by *trust* was that His people were not clinging to Him.

Moses was clinging and cleaving to God. He said unless You're going to go with me, I'm not going to go. He was afraid to go by himself. He woke up every day in fear of living apart from God. This is what the Hebrew word *devekut* means. It means cleaving and clinging to God and living in such a way that we would be afraid of taking a breath without Him.

Are you living a life of self-sufficiency? Do you need to be brought to your knees as Moses was when he said, "Unless You go with me, I will not go"? If so, ask the Lord to forgive you. Repent for being self-reliant, walking in presumption, and not starting each day by humbling yourself before Father God, letting Him know you're depending on Him and asking Him to be with you. Moses didn't dare walk presumptuously, assuming that everything would go well. He knew anything could go wrong outside God's favor and covering. He recognized that things would go well only as the Lord went before him.

The Bible tells us the accounts in the Old Testament were

written "as an example, and…for our instruction, upon whom the ends of the ages have come" (1 Cor. 10:11). Moses' life was an example for you and me. God used this humble man to lead a great army of people from bondage to freedom. When we assume the same posture of humility Moses took, we too can lay hold of God's promises and experience blessing, breakthrough, and abundant life in Yeshua.

Seek to Experience God's Glory

At the close of his prayer Moses said in verse 18, "Show me Your glory." Beloved, this is a prayer God wants to answer. He wants us to see His beauty and power, to know His divine intelligence and supernatural creativity. He wants us to know how marvelous He is. When Moses prayed, "Show me Your glory," he was saying, "God, show me how awesome and wondrous You are."

In the Gospel of John, Messiah Jesus imparted to us the glory that belonged to Him, and He prayed that we would dwell in and experience God's glory forever (John 17:22–24). This is God's purpose for us—to experience His glory. The Bible says, "For those whom He foreknew, He also predestined to become conformed to the image of His Son…and these whom He called, He also justified; and these whom He justified, He also glorified" (Rom. 8:29–30).

We have a glorious destiny in the Father, because God is the glorious One. He wants us to keep seeking His face—to keep knocking, to keep asking, and to keep praying as Moses prayed: "Lord, show me Your glory. Pour forth Your Spirit upon me. Pour forth Your love and joy on me. Reveal Yourself to me. Strengthen me." When we do, God will answer.

In the Cleft of the Rock

After Moses prayed, the Lord told him, "You can't see My face and live, but cover yourself in the cleft of the rock and call upon My name. As you do, I will come and proclaim My name to you." (See Exodus 33:20–23.) Then it happened!

As Moses called out to the Lord, Father God came and proclaimed His name, saying, "I am Yahweh, Yahweh God." Then He gave Moses a revelation of His essence, declaring that He is "the LORD God, compassionate and gracious, slow to anger, and abounding in lovingkindness and truth; who keeps lovingkindness for thousands, who forgives iniquity, transgression and sin; yet He will by no means leave the guilty unpunished" (Exod. 34:6–7).

After this encounter, Moses "made haste to bow low toward the earth and worship" (Exod. 34:8); then he asked the Lord to pardon the obstinance of the Israelites. God responded by renewing His covenant with His people and proclaiming that He would "perform miracles which have not been produced in all the earth nor among any of the nations" (Exod. 34:10).

Our cleft of the rock is Jesus. Even as Moses called upon God to reveal His glory from the cleft in the rock, you and I can call upon Father God to reveal His glory to us through Yeshua. When we do, Messiah Jesus will bring us into a deeper and fuller awareness of who He is, cause us to experience His glory by His Spirit, and transform us by His power.

We know that in this life, we see through a glass dimly, that "eye has not seen, nor ear heard, nor has it entered into the heart of man the things which God has prepared for those who love Him" (1 Cor. 2:9, MEV). But as we follow Jesus, we are being brought more and more into a discovery of God's fullness. We don't have to wait until we die and go to heaven to experience the glory of God. When we leave our bodies, we're going to experience God's glory in a way we'll never experience fully on this earth. But even while we're in the flesh, we can experience the glory of God, just as Moses did.

Yeshua said those who follow Him have eternal life, and eternal life is an experience! Many people think of eternal life in terms of time. They think it is about living forever. By all means when we receive eternal life through Yeshua, we live forever. But Jesus said, "This is eternal life, that they may know You, the only true God, and Jesus Christ whom You have sent" (John 17:3). Relationship and experience are characteristics of eternal life.

That is why I am passionate about Yeshua—because I am experiencing Him in the here and now. Am I experiencing Him as much as I would like to? No. I still hunger and yearn for more— much more—but Jesus is making Himself real to me. Messiah Jesus said, "Blessed are those who hunger and thirst for righteousness, for they shall be satisfied" (Matt. 5:6). He will make Himself known to anyone who hungers and thirsts for Him.

I pray that you will encounter God's glory in this season in a way that brings massive transformation to your life. Messiah Jesus said if we believe, we will see the glory of God (John 11:40). So beloved, reach out to Him in love, knowing that He is reaching back to you.

⚘

Keep asking Yeshua to show Himself to you. Paul prayed that God would give us a spirit of wisdom and revelation in the knowledge of Him (Eph. 1:17). Whenever you have a revelation of the knowledge of God, you have an experience of the glory of God.

Request of Father God, "Do for me what You did for Moses. Show me Your glory. Let me know Your love and favor on my life. I humbly rely on You."

Chapter 4

THE FATHER'S PRAYER OVER US

The LORD bless you, and keep you; the LORD make His
face shine on you, and be gracious to you; the LORD
lift up His countenance on you, and give you peace.
—NUMBERS 6:24–26

I N THE BOOK of Numbers, God gave Moses specific instructions for how to bless the children of Israel.

Then the LORD spoke to Moses, saying, "Speak to Aaron and to his sons, saying, 'Thus you shall bless the sons of Israel. You shall say to them: The LORD bless you, and keep you; the LORD make His face shine on you, and be gracious to you; the LORD lift up His countenance on you, and give you peace.' So they shall invoke My name on the sons of Israel, and I then will bless them."
—NUMBERS 6:22–27

Called the Priestly or Aaronic Blessing, this prayer is brief, but it is filled with deep spiritual meaning. In this chapter we will walk through each line of this powerful prayer, learning from the Hebrew what Father God wants us to know about His love, power, and goodness toward us, His children.

Written by God

What I love so much about this blessing is it didn't originate with man. The words of this prayer actually proceeded from the very essence of God Himself.

In the Old Testament whenever we see Lord rendered in capital letters, it actually represents the original Hebrew letters *yud, hey, vav, hey*—YHWH. Most Semitic scholars believe it is pronounced as a breathy "Yah-weh." This is God's personal, covenant name. The fact that God revealed it to us and actually uses it in this blessing assures us that this blessing is coming not from some anonymous god in the sky but from a personal God who actually has a name.

God told Moses, "I appeared to Abraham, Isaac, and Jacob, as God Almighty [a title], but by My name [Yahweh] I did not make Myself known to them" (Exod. 6:3). By using His personal, covenant name as He pronounces these blessings over us, God is revealing Himself not just as Lord, which is a somewhat impersonal title, but as Yahweh, our loving Father.

Consider this also: A noun is often described as a person, place, or thing, and oftentimes we think of nouns as being static. Yahweh is a person, but He is beyond a noun because He is not static. In fact, He is a living being whose life flows in continual, present action. So understand that when the words of this prayer are being spoken, this is not dead liturgy. This is the covenant-keeping God continually applying this blessing over His people by His Spirit through His Son.

When God gave this blessing to Moses, He told him to "speak to Aaron and to his sons, saying, 'Thus you shall bless the sons of Israel'" (Num. 6:23). Although this prayer is often called the Aaronic Blessing, it didn't originate with Aaron and his sons, who had been consecrated priests. They were just God's agents. Again, the Lord Himself gave the blessing. He told Aaron and his sons, "This is what I want you to say over My people, My chosen ones." This means this prayer is for you. If you belong to Jesus, you are one of God's chosen ones. The blessing Father God spoke over ancient Israel He speaks over your life today in Messiah Yeshua because we, Jew and Gentile, have become one in Christ and the whole church is the Israel of God.

Please don't misunderstand. I'm not saying Gentiles are now Jews. I'm saying that in a prophetic sense the church is now the Israel of God (Gal. 6:15–16). The church has not replaced Israel, but in a spiritual sense the whole church is God's chosen people, for "by one Spirit we were all baptized into one body, whether Jews or Greeks" (1 Cor. 12:13).

This blessing then was not meant only for ancient Israel. It is for you, beloved, and by faith you can gain revelation of who God is and how He feels about you, and incorporate this blessing into your prayer life.

A Blessing From Yahweh

Of all the prayers we examine in this book, this is the only one spoken directly by God. We can know that the blessings contained in what we call the Aaronic Blessing are for us to receive because Father Himself pronounced them.

Let's open our hearts and receive Father's blessing. The first line declares, "Yahweh bless you and keep you." (*"Y'varekh'kha*

Yahweh v'yishmerekha.") The Hebrew word translated "bless you" is *y'varekh'kha,* and it presents a word picture of a king stooping down and presenting a gift to one of his subjects. This word captures God's love, favor, and grace. It reflects His disposition toward us as the One who blesses us. He stooped down to love, bless, and receive you and me right where we are.

The Hebrew word translated "keep you" or "protect you" is *v'yishmerekha.* This word paints a picture of a shepherd, like the ones described in Scripture, corralling his sheep to protect them. Remember, Messiah Jesus is the Good Shepherd, who guards His sheep. "Not one of them perished but the son of perdition, so that the Scripture would be fulfilled" (John 17:12).

We live in a world that is full of dangers all around. We read of sickness, suicide, war, disease, car accidents, natural disasters, pandemics, global warming, hate, murders, and all types of things that would, in the natural, incite fear. But God is saying to you, "You don't have to fear. I, Yahweh, your Father, am with you. I am protecting you and will keep you."

The Scripture says in Isaiah 8:12–14:

> You are not to say, "It is a conspiracy!" in regard to all that this people call a conspiracy, and you are not to fear what they fear or be in dread of it. It is the LORD of hosts whom you should regard as holy. And He shall be your fear, and He shall be your dread. Then He shall become a sanctuary.

In effect what the Lord is saying here is, "Don't fear what the world fears, for I alone am to be your God. Fear me alone. I am protecting you from all these things."

So when we read *"Y'varekh'kha Yahweh"* ("the Lord bless

you") *"v'yishmerekha"* ("and protect you"), we should take confidence and know the Lord is protecting us. I pray you receive this deep in your spirit: God has blessed you, is blessing you, and will bless you. And you are protected by a personal God who created you and rules over everything, so don't fear.

The blessing continues in Numbers 6:25: "The LORD make His face shine on you, and be gracious to you." (*"Ya'er Yahweh panav eleikha vichunekka."*) The words *panav eleikha* used in this statement mean face. In other words, the Lord's face is toward you and me. He is looking at us with eyes of love. His face is shining on us. His strength, glory, goodness, and love are directed toward us. As we keep our eyes on Him, He imparts His very essence, nature, and power unto us. To echo the apostle Paul, "I pray that the eyes of your heart may be enlightened, so that you will know what is the hope of His calling, what are the riches of the glory of His inheritance in the saints, *and what is the surpassing greatness of His power toward us who believe"* (Eph. 1:18–19, emphasis added).

In the next phrase we hear the pronouncement of divine grace over our lives: "and be gracious to you." The term translated "gracious" (*vichunekka*) carries the idea, once again, of a king stooping down in kindness, mercy, and tenderness toward an inferior. It conveys the sense that because of His power, God could smash us with His fists if He wanted to, but He does the exact opposite. He stoops down to be kind and gracious to us, though we've done nothing to earn or deserve it. Receive this. Father sent His Son to die for us while we were yet sinners. He wasn't legally obligated to do this. His grace, His desire to give us His love, His *chesed* (the Hebrew word for *grace, compassion,* and *kindness*) moved Him.

For one will hardly die for a righteous man; though perhaps for the good man someone would dare even to die. But God demonstrates His own love toward us, in that while we were yet sinners, Christ died for us. Much more then, having now been justified by His blood, we shall be saved from the wrath of God through Him.

—ROMANS 5:7–9

But God, being rich in mercy, because of His great love with which He loved us, even when we were dead in our transgressions, made us alive together with Christ (by grace you have been saved), and raised us up with Him, and seated us with Him in the heavenly places in Christ Jesus, so that in the ages to come He might show the surpassing riches of His grace in kindness toward us in Christ Jesus. For by grace you have been saved through faith; and that not of yourselves, it is the gift of God.

—EPHESIANS 2:4–8

In Numbers 6:26 the blessing goes on to say, "The LORD lift up His countenance on you." ("*Yissa Yahweh panav eleikha.*") This statement communicates the idea of a father lifting up his baby and beaming as he gazes at his child. This is how God feels about us. It's hard for many of us to comprehend that God simply delights in us. But let's remember that He created us in His own image to have a relationship with Him, and there's something in us that is so valuable to Him that He sent Messiah Jesus, His Son, to die on the cross for us and purchase us by His blood.

Do you believe that? Beloved, God loved you before you ever knew Jesus. That's why He sent Yeshua. The Father loved you and me so much that He sent Messiah Jesus to die for us and bring us back to Him. Now He holds us up like a father proudly lifting up his child, just beaming with adoration. I know this is hard for many to understand, but this is how Father God feels about you and me. He loves and delights in us.

Paul prayed for us in Ephesians 1:18, that we would be enlightened to understand "the riches of the glory of His inheritance in the saints." It is often very difficult for us to understand the value God has given us in His heart. We think, "How can God delight in me?" The realm of darkness that encircles the earth has projected such accusation against us that we have difficulty seeing ourselves as beautiful to God. We struggle to understand how we can bring Him pleasure, how He could be happy with us, or how we can bring Him delight. But somehow we do! Remember, the angels in heaven rejoice over every person who turns to God. Jesus said, "In the same way, I tell you, there is joy in the presence of the angels of God over one sinner who repents" (Luke 15:10).

Father, Yeshua, and the Holy Spirit are with us, continually fellowshipping with us through every detail of our journeys. There isn't one thought that you think that God doesn't feel. Father and Yeshua have joy in you.

The Lord gave me a window into understanding this some years ago when a good friend of mine told me about a dream she had had about me. In the dream I was playing baseball and hitting the ball out of the park, hitting home runs. And she said she felt Father's joy over me as He was watching me. But she said it wasn't so much that He was rejoicing that I was hitting home runs. Rather, His joy was in experiencing me loving the game so much. In other words, Father was taking pleasure in seeing me enjoying myself.

I remember taking my two-and-a-half-year-old grand-daughter to see Christmas lights. We drove through the Columbus Zoo, where they had a huge light show. I opened the roof of the vehicle and let her stand on the console so her head was out the roof of the car, and she was so excited seeing the lights. It is one of my most precious memories of being with her. It was so fulfilling seeing her so excited and happy. Somehow the Lord relates to us in the same way. I know it's mind-bending, but it's truth.

The prayer ends by saying, "...and give you peace" ("...*v'yasem l'kha shalom*"). This is the blessing of *shalom*.

The Hebrew word *shalom*, which is where the word *peace* comes from, means complete wholeness. It's not just the absence of conflict. *Shalom* means complete wholeness—spirit, soul, mind, and body. Because of the powers of darkness that surround the spiritual atmosphere we live in (Rev. 2:13), we struggle with brokenness, self-rejection, and the inability to receive God's offer of *shalom* (wholeness). We feel unworthy, guilty, and ashamed. Like Adam and Eve, who ran from God because of their guilt and shame, so too we often find it difficult to receive from God because of our own self-rejection.

After Adam and Eve yielded to Satan and the realm of darkness, we read that "the eyes of both of them were opened, and they knew that they were naked; and they sewed fig leaves together and made themselves loin coverings. They heard the sound of the LORD God walking in the garden in the cool of the day, and the man and his wife hid themselves from the presence of the LORD God among the trees of the garden" (Gen. 3:7–8). They didn't run to God; they ran from Him. They couldn't even be comfortable with themselves anymore. They felt self-conscious, naked, and bad about themselves. They tried to cover their sense of discomfort in their own skin with fig leaves.

To receive His forgiveness and *shalom*, we have to reject the spirit of shame, guilt, and self-rejection and the mindset that seeks to run from God rather than turn to Him. The Lord wants to heal us and make us whole and complete in Him. This is what God desires for you and me—that we would have peace, walk in wholeness, and be complete in Yeshua. Scripture says, "In Him [Jesus] you have been made complete" (Col. 2:10).

The gift that God has given us, His kids, is His own completeness, His own *shalom*. When Yeshua revealed Himself to His disciples after He rose from the dead, He said, "My *shalom*, My peace, I give to you." Then He breathed on them and said, "Receive the Holy Spirit." (See John 20:19–22.) In another passage, Yeshua said, "In Me you may have peace. In the world you will have tribulation. But be of good cheer. I have overcome the world" (John 16:33, MEV).

Please hear me: The Aaronic Blessing is not just a poetic pleasantry. It is not wishful thinking. It is not like a greeting card that's full of nice, trite sayings. This prayer comes from the essence of God's heart. The Lord desires that we walk confidently in these truths. He wants us to know we are blessed and safe in this dark and dangerous world.

Father God is always looking at you and me. We're never outside of His love. We're never outside of His care. We're never outside of His protection. Twenty-four hours a day, seven days a week, every second the clock ticks, He's looking at you and me. We're protected, blessed, and safe in Him because He's holding us!

We need to understand that God delights in us. That is why Paul tells us we should pray to understand the riches of the glory of God's inheritance in the saints (Eph. 1:18). We need to ask Him for revelation so we can understand how valuable and precious we are to Him. Do you want to pray prayers that God will answer? Keep praying for the fulfillment of what Father God has blessed you with in this prayer. In due course He will answer.

Receive It by Faith

Now let's read Exodus 6:24–26 again in the present tense, and this time receive it by faith.

"I, the Lord who has become your Father through My Son, Yeshua, am blessing you and keeping you."

Doesn't that make you feel safe? Doesn't it give you a positive outlook on your life to know that right now God Himself, your Father, has blessed you and will continue to bless you going forward and that He is keeping you?

"I, Yahweh the Lord, am making My face shine on you."

Beloved, there is favor on your life. Wherever you go, Father God is looking at you to favor and bless you. If we receive this disposition, we're going to move mountains in this world because we'll be walking in the confidence that God Himself is with us. Remember, Jesus said to us, "I am with you always, even to the end of the age" (Matt. 28:20). That's what we're receiving when we declare and pray those words. God's favor is always with and upon us.

"I am being gracious to you."

Again, this statement includes the Hebrew word *vichunekka*, which describes a king stooping down to present a gift to someone he loves, someone who is his inferior. The person has no claim on anything; the king does this simply because he is dispositioned to love and be kind to this individual.

This is God's attitude toward you and me. He has come down to where we are. ~~Messiah Jesus, who is God Himself, lowered Himself to become a man~~, clothed Himself in flesh and blood, and died on the cross for us. He stooped down to us. Why? Because He wanted to! He sees only good in you because He has forgiven and removed your sin. He has made you His righteousness in Christ. As the apostle Paul wrote, "By His doing you are in Christ Jesus, who became to us wisdom from God, and righteousness and sanctification, and redemption" (1 Cor. 1:30).

"I am lifting up My countenance on you."

This is, once again, the idea of a father lifting up a child and just beaming with joy and pride. God accepts you. To "lift up His countenance on you" is to bring you into His presence, into His heart. He enjoys you and me and longs to be in relationship with us. God has chosen to give us such a special place in His heart. He lifts up His countenance on us, inviting us into fellowship with Him.

His kindness, goodness, and favor are here for you. But will you believe ~~Him, receive Him, and let Him in? Jesu~~s said, "Behold, I stand at the door and knock; if anyone hears My voice and opens the door, I will come in to him and will dine with him, and he with Me" (Rev. 3:20).

"And I'm giving you My peace."

Again, the Hebrew word *shalom* ~~means peace~~ and completeness. Yeshua said the *shalom* He imparts to His own is not of this world. The type of peace that Messiah Yeshua gives is independent and not tied to circumstances. He gives peace in the spirit realm. When you think about it, our circumstances are not the real problem. The way we think about and view our circumstances—that is where the battle for peace is. One person faces a severe challenge and falls into depression, hopelessness, or fear. Another person faces the same exact challenge, and although it is difficult, the person is excited about the spiritual growth he or she will receive by going through the challenge while clinging to God. It's the same challenge, but one person gives up and another is excited about what God is going to do in his or her life and presses through. The one had *shalom*; the other didn't, but the circumstance was the same.

Jesus said, "Peace I leave with you; My peace I give to you; not as the world gives do I give to you. Do not let your heart be troubled, nor let it be fearful" (John 14:27). Father through Yeshua by His Spirit is strengthening us so that we will no longer be the victims of circumstances in the material, visible world. He has called us to a higher realm, a spiritual realm of peace and victory that transcends our circumstances.

Jesus stood before Pilate fearless (Matt. 27:11–14). Paul rejoiced in prison (Acts 16:16–40). Stephen stood full of the Holy Spirit and saw God's glory as he was being stoned to death (Acts 7:54–60). The peace that Father desires to bless us with empowers us to live in His light, victory, presence, and *shalom* through all our circumstances for the rest of our lives. Paul wrote, "Who will separate us from the love of Christ? Will tribulation, or distress, or persecution, or famine, or nakedness, or peril, or sword? Just as it is written, 'For Your sake we are being put to death all day long; we were considered as sheep to be slaughtered.' But in all these things we overwhelmingly conquer through Him who loved us. For I am convinced that neither death, nor life, nor angels, nor principalities, nor things present, nor things to come, nor powers, nor height, nor depth, nor any other created thing, will be able to separate us from the love of God, which is in Christ Jesus our Lord" (Rom. 8:35–39).

~≪≪≪~

Y'varekh'kha Yahweh v'yishmerekha. Ya'er Yahweh panav eleikha vichunekka. Yissa Yahweh panav eleikha v'yasem l'kha shalom. ("Yahweh bless you and keep you. Yahweh make His face shine on you and be gracious to you. Yahweh lift up His countenance on you and give you peace.")

I want to encourage you to receive this blessing. We who are in His Son don't have to wonder if God likes and loves us. We don't have to wonder if He is blessing us. We don't have to wonder whether His favor is on us. It is. Scripture says, "Grace to you and peace from God our Father and the Lord Jesus Christ. Blessed be the God and Father of our Lord Jesus Christ, who has blessed us with every spiritual blessing in the heavenly places in Christ" (Eph. 1:2–3). Believe it, walk in it, and receive it.

PART II

Kings and Prophets: The Bold and the Wise

Chapter 5

A PRAYER FOR WISDOM

Then Solomon said, "...Now, O LORD my God, You
have made Your servant king in place of my father
David, yet I am but a little child....So give Your
servant an understanding heart to judge Your
people to discern between good and evil."
—1 KINGS 3:6–7, 9

N OT LONG AFTER David's son Solomon was anointed
as king, he went to Gibeon to make sacrifices to God,
and an amazing thing happened. While he was there,
the Lord appeared to him in a dream and said, "Ask what you
wish Me to give you" (1 Kings 3:5).

Can you imagine hearing God say something like that to you?
No limitations—ask anything you want. Many people would
seek money or success, love or long life, and those requests have
their place. But those things weren't at the top of Solomon's list.

Then Solomon said, "You have shown great lovingkindness
to Your servant David my father, according as he walked

49

before You in truth and righteousness and uprightness of heart toward You; and You have reserved for him this great lovingkindness, that You have given him a son to sit on his throne, as it is this day. Now, O LORD my God, You have made Your servant king in place of my father David, yet I am but a little child; I do not know how to go out or come in. Your servant is in the midst of Your people which You have chosen, a great people who are too many to be numbered or counted. So give Your servant an understanding heart to judge Your people to discern between good and evil. For who is able to judge this great people of Yours?"

—1 KINGS 3:6–9

What an incredible lesson we can learn from Solomon through this prayer. Above all else Solomon asked for wisdom. This is what the Book of Proverbs admonishes us over and over to seek. Proverbs 4:7 tells us to "acquire wisdom; and with all your acquiring, get understanding." And we read in Proverbs 3:13, "How blessed is the man who finds wisdom." Wisdom, however, isn't described in Proverbs simply as a series of correct values we must understand. Proverbs speaks of wisdom as a person (Prov. 8:12, 14), and that person is Yeshua, "who became to us wisdom from God" (1 Cor. 1:30).

This is what Solomon sought in his prayer—a dynamic insight and understanding of reality from God's perspective so he could rule correctly. Israel's young king didn't ask for superficial things. He didn't first ask for riches or honor. He didn't begin by asking for protection from his enemies. Again, those things sometimes have their place, but Solomon sought something deeper. He asked for something more important to the heart of God, something that would allow him to lead others in the right way. He asked for wisdom, which is the very person of Jesus.

This pleased God so much He gave Solomon even more than he asked for.

> God said to him, "Because you have asked this thing and have not asked for yourself long life, nor have asked riches for yourself, nor have you asked for the life of your enemies, but have asked for yourself discernment to understand justice, behold, I have done according to your words. Behold, I have given you a wise and discerning heart, so that there has been no one like you before you, nor shall one like you arise after you. I have also given you what you have not asked, both riches and honor, so that there will not be any among the kings like you all your days."
>
> —1 KINGS 3:11–13

This is why it is so important to ask God for the things that really matter to Him. Some prayers carry more weight with God than others. Some requests please the Father more than others.

If you have children or grandchildren, doesn't it please you when they ask you for things that show they have right values? Maybe they want to spend time with you, or perhaps they ask for your help with something or advice. Doesn't that please you a lot more than when they beg you for the latest toy or video game or some other temporal thing?

Years ago one of my daughters said, "Daddy, whenever we do something, it's always with both me and Alyssa [her sister]. Can we do something together, just you and me alone?" My daughter is now an adult with a family of her own, but her request still touches my heart; I still remember it after all these years.

We know, then, from our relationships with our children and grandchildren that some of the things they ask for from us are more meaningful than others. It is the same with our heavenly Father. Our prayers can move God's heart. What we seek will determine how He responds to us and how much pleasure He gets from our communication with Him. Solomon's desire for wisdom moved God's heart far more than if he had asked for riches, fame, or honor. And because Solomon's prayer was so pleasing to the Father, God incredibly blessed him, marking him as the wisest man who would ever live.

> Now God gave Solomon wisdom and very great discernment and breadth of mind, like the sand that is on the seashore. Solomon's wisdom surpassed the wisdom of all the sons of the east and all the wisdom of Egypt. For he was wiser than all men...and his fame was known in all the surrounding nations. He also spoke 3,000 proverbs, and his songs were 1,005. He spoke of trees, from the cedar that is in Lebanon even to the hyssop that grows on the wall; he spoke also of animals and birds and creeping things and fish. Men came from all peoples to hear the wisdom of Solomon, from all the kings of the earth who had heard of his wisdom.
>
> —1 KINGS 4:29–34

We All Need Wisdom

How deeply we all need wisdom. Unfortunately and sadly, many people look to this world for wisdom, thinking they will find it in education, technology, or philosophy. But seeking wisdom from the world is futile, for God has "made foolish the wisdom of the world" (1 Cor. 1:20). Scripture says that in Messiah Jesus "are hidden all the treasures of wisdom and knowledge" (Col. 2:3). True wisdom comes only from God.

If we want to be good husbands, wives, employers, employees, neighbors, parents, or grandparents, we must ask Father God for wisdom. If we want to carry ourselves in a way that reflects and imparts God's glory to those in our sphere of influence, we need to ask the Lord for wisdom.

Proverbs 4:7 says, "Wisdom is the principal thing; therefore get wisdom: and with all thy getting get understanding" (kjv). Beloved, it takes wisdom to understand what is really happening in life. It takes wisdom to understand the deeper nature of things.

Scripture says the Lord gave Solomon "a wise and discerning heart" (1 Kings 3:12). It takes wisdom to successfully navigate life. So many people go through life being taken advantage of because they don't have wise and discerning hearts. Don't you want to be able to see through situations, to discern people's motives, to glimpse the end of a matter? Don't you want wisdom as you make decisions at home, at work, and in your relationships? Don't you want wisdom to plan for the future? God wants you to ask Him for this.

The Book of Proverbs says by wisdom "your days will be multiplied, and years of life will be added to you" (Prov. 9:11). Wisdom will deliver to you a crown of glory (Prov. 4:9). So beloved, seek wisdom. Make it a priority in your prayer life with Father, Yeshua, and the Holy Spirit. And don't stop after just one prayer. Jesus said, "Ask and keep on asking and it will be given to you; seek and keep on seeking and you will find; knock and keep on knocking and the door will be opened to you" (Matt. 7:7, amp). If you keep knocking and keep asking for wisdom, He's going to give it to you.

Scripture says, "You do not have because you do not ask" (Jas. 4:2). If you pray a little, you will receive a little. Jesus said, "Ask and you will receive, so that your joy may be made full" (John 16:24). So I want to inspire you to ask the Lord for wisdom, just as Solomon did.

When you get up in the morning, don't rush first to check your phone or emails. Don't text or talk to anybody. Let the first part of your day be set apart for God. Sit down before Him on your couch or chair or whatever place you choose. Designate a special place to spend time with Him. Ask Father God if you dreamed anything the night before that He wants you to remember. Seek Him for understanding and revelation. Then read a chapter slowly from the Scriptures. Read devotionals. My wife, Cynthia, has written one titled *From Passover to Pentecost*, which I believe is very good. There are many good ones out there. Read what the Holy Spirit leads you to read—feed yourself the Word.

Then talk to God. Tell Him what's on your heart. Ask Him to reveal Himself to you. Ask Him for help in the areas where you're struggling. Ask Him to strengthen you with the same power that raised Jesus from the dead. Ask Him to give you a spirit of revelation in the knowledge of Him. Ask Him to help you discern His power and leading in your life. And ask Him for wisdom. As you keep asking, you will receive. Yeshua said, "Everyone who asks receives, and he who seeks finds, and to him who knocks it will be opened" (Matt. 7:8). As you seek His wisdom, you're going to become smarter and smarter and more and more discerning.

Beloved, I want to encourage you to believe God for more. Father God has good plans for you and me. He wants to give us wisdom. He answered Solomon's prayer for a wise and discerning heart, and you can be assured He will answer you too.

Chapter 6

A CRY TO KNOW GOD

Make me know Your ways, O LORD; teach me Your paths.
Lead me in Your truth and teach me, for You are the God of
my salvation; for You I wait all the day....Do not remember
the sins of my youth or my transgressions....Turn to me
and be gracious to me, for I am lonely and afflicted.
—PSALM 25:4–5, 7, 16

DAVID IS WELL-KNOWN as the shepherd boy who killed
Goliath and later became one of Israel's greatest kings.
But he also wrote most of the poems and songs in the
Book of Psalms. He was not ashamed to pour his heart out to
the Lord. In fact, David walked so closely with God that the
Lord called him "a man after My heart" (Acts 13:22). Jesus
said He is "the root and the descendant of David" (Rev. 22:16).
Yeshua also described Himself as the One who holds the key of
David (Rev. 3:7), which I believe is intimacy with God.

Father God loved David deeply, and I believe He drew close
to him because David's heart was in the proper posture before
Him. The most common and traditional Hebrew word for

prayer is *tefillah*, and it has to do with putting oneself in proper alignment with the Creator. We see this act of spiritual alignment in physical form when Orthodox Jews pray at the Western Wall in Jerusalem, swaying back and forth. This is called davening and refers to the Spirit of the Lord being like a flame that moves within us. It is symbolic of putting oneself in a correct posture before the Lord.

This is what David did again and again. He was far from perfect, but he was quick to run to Father God in prayer, worship, and repentance. As a result, David was a man who walked closely with God. So what did someone known for his intimacy with God seek in prayer? There is much we can learn from David's petition in Psalm 25.

In verses 4 and 5 David prayed, "Make me know Your ways, O LORD; teach me Your paths. Lead me in Your truth and teach me, for You are the God of my salvation; for You I wait all the day." What an awesome cry from the heart of a king! So many today pray for superficial things, asking to be blessed with a new job, new car, or new house. But that wasn't David's request. He wanted to understand the very mind and ways of God.

Yes, material things are important, and I'm so thankful that Father God blesses us with those things, but He is most concerned about the deeper issues of the heart. Jesus said, "Do not worry then, saying, 'What will we eat?' or 'What will we drink?' or 'What will we wear for clothing?'...But seek first His kingdom and His righteousness, and all these things will be added to you" (Matt. 6:31, 33). Where is the kingdom of God? According to Yeshua, it is within us (Luke 17:21).

There's no question, if you ask the Lord to teach you His ways, He's going to do it. You don't have to wonder whether He will or won't. He will because you're praying according to His will for you. He wants to teach you His ways. When you ask God to guide you in His path, the path of salvation, and you really mean it and keep seeking Him for it, He's going to do that for you.

When we ask some things of the Lord, we don't know for sure how He's going to respond because we don't know His will about those things. We may ask the Lord to give us a certain job, but unless He has spoken to us specifically about that position, we don't know for sure that He wants us to have it. There are many athletes who pray for their team to win the big game. Players on one team get on their knees and pray, "God, please give us the victory today," and players on the opposing team do the same. But we don't know what God is going to do in that situation. We don't know which team is going to win the game.

But when we pray for the things God wants to bring forth from our innermost beings, when we pray about those realities, we can have complete confidence that not only is God going to hear, but He's also going to answer. And not only is He going to answer; He's going to add everything else unto us, just as Yeshua said.

A Supernatural Mindset

In his prayer David asked to know the mind and ways of God. You may be wondering what that means. Jesus said the Lord is looking for those who will worship Him in spirit and truth (John 4:24). So if we want to know the ways of God, as David prayed, we have to know Him according to the Spirit because God is Spirit, and spirit by definition is supernatural. That is why one of the things involved in knowing the mind and ways of God is developing a supernatural mindset.

When we have a supernatural mindset, our thinking isn't based on the natural realm, or on what we see. We think above the natural. In Mark 11 the disciples marveled when Jesus cursed the fig tree and all the leaves withered. Jesus said, "Truly I say to you, whoever says to this mountain, 'Be taken up and cast into the sea,' and does not doubt in his heart, but believes that what he says is going to happen, it will be granted him. Therefore I say to you, all things for which you pray and ask, believe that you have received them, and they will be granted you" (vv. 23–24). That's the kind of mindset Jesus is calling us to have—one that is supernatural.

Too many of us are walking around limited by the natural. We are stuck in our own ways of thinking and are missing out on the joy and freedom we can have through Messiah Jesus. We'll never know Father God's ways if we live according to a natural mindset. "For the mind set on the flesh is death, but the mind set on the Spirit is life and peace, because the mind set on the flesh is hostile toward God; for it does not subject itself to the law of God, for it is not even able to do so, and those who are in the flesh cannot please God" (Rom. 8:6–8). This is why Scripture says we are to be transformed by the renewing of our minds through the Word of God (Rom. 12:2).

One of the ways we lift ourselves above the natural to walk in the supernatural is by confessing God's Word. We don't confess the natural; we confess the supernatural. We remind ourselves, "I can do all things through [Christ] who strengthens me" (Phil. 4:13). We declare that we shall know the truth in Jesus and the truth is setting us free (John 8:32). We don't confess the limitations of our circumstances; we confess the eternal Word of God—that we have been raised with Christ and are seated with Him in the heavenly places (Eph. 2:6) and that our real life, identity, and purpose is "hidden with Christ in God" (Col. 3:3). Circumstances and what people think of us do not define us. God through Messiah does.

That is the kind of life Yeshua demonstrated. He didn't live according to the natural. He walked on the water. He multiplied the loaves and the fish to feed thousands. He took authority over sickness and disease. He told His disciples if they were bitten by a deadly serpent, it wouldn't hurt them. (See Mark 16:17–18.) In the natural the disciples would have gotten sick and likely died if they had been bitten by a poisonous snake. But in Messiah Jesus we are not limited by the natural.

In Acts 28, when the apostle Paul was bitten by a poisonous snake while gathering wood for a fire, the locals thought it was a sign he was cursed. They assumed he would get sick, maybe even die. Instead, Paul shook off the snake, and its venom had no effect on him. When the people saw that the snakebite didn't hurt Paul, they began to think he was a god. Paul took that opportunity to share the gospel. That is what Jesus was talking about when He said those who believe in His name will be bitten by deadly serpents and not be harmed. He was talking about living a supernatural life!

Our God is a supernatural God, and we see Him working supernaturally throughout Scripture. He began by creating the heavens and the earth out of nothing. Then He parted the Red Sea for the children of Israel to walk across it without being harmed. When they got into the wilderness, there was no food. What did God do? He supernaturally provided manna for them six days a week for forty years. As if that weren't enough, God came down in fire and glory on Mount Sinai. Approximately three million Israelites who were gathered at the base of the mountain heard God speak from heaven. That's supernatural!

In the story of Daniel in the lions' den, God supernaturally shut the lions' mouths. When Shadrach, Meshach, and Abednego were thrown in the fiery furnace, God supernaturally protected them so they weren't burned. In fact, when they were released, they didn't even smell like smoke.

In the New Testament we read of Jesus walking on water, multiplying the fish and the loaves to feed a multitude, and telling His disciples to cast their nets on the other side, which led to them catching so many fish their nets couldn't hold them all. Our entire faith is based on the supernatural because our faith rests on Jesus rising from the dead, and that's supernatural!

Perhaps you think, "Yeah, I read those stories in the Bible, but God did that kind of thing thousands of years ago. Miracles like that don't happen anymore." Beloved, God's ways are eternal, and He's doing the same thing in the lives of His children today as He did thousands of years ago. And not only that. Jesus said, "He who believes in Me, the works that I do, he will do also; and greater works than these he will do; because I go to the Father" (John 14:12).

God is supernatural, and the only way to walk with Him is to realize there is more to life than what we see. The Bible says, "We look not at the things which are seen, but at the things which are not seen; for the things which are seen are temporal, but the things which are not seen are eternal" (2 Cor. 4:18). "Therefore if you have been raised up with Christ, keep seeking the things above, where Christ is, seated at the right hand of

God. Set your mind on the things above, not on the things that are on earth" (Col. 3:1–2). The things of this world are temporary and fading away. The unseen and supernatural things, they are what are lasting and real.

David said to the Lord, "Teach me Your ways." Beloved, if we want to know God's ways, we need to start developing a confidence in the unseen truths of His Spirit. We need to start believing Him for more than what the material world around us is telling us is possible. Jesus said, "Truly I say to you, whoever says to this mountain, 'Be taken up and cast into the sea,' and does not doubt in his heart, but believes that what he says is going to happen, it will be granted him" (Mark 11:23). "All things are possible to him who believes" (Mark 9:23).

According to His Lovingkindness

David was not only concerned with God teaching him His ways; he prayed in verse 7, "Do not remember the sins of my youth or my transgressions; according to Your lovingkindness remember me, for Your goodness' sake, O Lord" (Ps. 25:7). It is my prayer that through the heart of David you will see Father God's desire to forgive His children and show us mercy. Perhaps you still struggle at times with things you did in the past. Beloved, I want you to know today that it is God's heart to forgive you of past sins. Think of all the sins David committed, not the least of which were murder and adultery. He wasn't a perfect man, but he loved God and pursued Him, and his God forgave him for his sins.

Our God is compassionate and gracious by nature. (See Exodus 34:6–7.) Reject the enemy's accusations and his attempts to heap guilt and shame on you because of mistakes from your past. The Bible says, "Therefore there is now no condemnation for those who are in Christ Jesus. For the law of the Spirit of life in Christ Jesus has set you free from the law of sin and of death" (Rom. 8:1–2).

When we repent as David did, Scripture says God casts our sins into the sea of forgetfulness (Mic. 7:19). And we read in Psalms that "as far as the east is from the west, so far has He removed our transgressions from us" (Ps. 103:12). In Messiah Jesus, though our "sins are as scarlet, they will be as white as snow; though they are red like crimson, they will be like wool" (Isa. 1:18). This is God's promise to you and me, but Satan doesn't want us to grab hold of this truth. He wants us to think our past sins are too much for God to forgive, that because of our failings, He is withdrawing His presence and leaving us to face life on our own. But that is not true. Beloved, you have been forgiven, God is with you, and you never have to feel alone.

David prayed in Psalm 25:16, "Turn to me and be gracious to me, for I am lonely and afflicted." When David felt lonely, he reached out to Father God and said, "Lord, I'm lonely. Let me feel Your presence. Come and comfort me." We can do the same. When we're lonely, we can pray, "Jesus, put Your hand on my heart and touch me. Help me to know You're with me. Cause me to feel Your presence. Help me to know how much You love me. Let me feel Your kiss on my heart, Yeshua." That is a prayer God wants to answer—He wants you to experience His embrace.

Perhaps you've been widowed or never married and you're feeling alone. Even if you're married, the only One who can truly fill loneliness is the Lord. So if you need the Lord to touch you, don't be ashamed. Do what David did and pray, "Lord, be gracious to me, for I'm lonely and afflicted." Just as Father God in Yeshua was very tender with David, so too He can be tender with you. David said to the Lord in Psalm 18:35, "Your gentleness makes me great." Beloved, Father is closer to you and me than our own breath. If you keep asking Him, He will cause you to sense His presence.

Messiah Jesus said, "I am with you always, even to the end of the age" (Matt. 28:20). Ask your Creator to open your heart to truly understand this, to truly know how much He loves you and how close He is to you. He wants to envelop us in His presence. We too can pray that God will release His manifest presence upon our lives.

~~~~~

Beloved, we learn from Psalm 25 that God wants to teach us His ways. He wants to forgive you and show you mercy. He wants you to realize that He is closer to you than anyone in this world will ever be. And He wants you to live above the natural. Boldly ask the Lord to help you do this. Ask Him to show you His ways. Ask Him to give you a supernatural mindset. And ask Him to help you know He is always with you. Then confess those realities.

As you pray as David did, you will come to know Father God's ways, experience His goodness, and realize you are never alone, because if you ask anything according to His will, He hears you and you have the request that you have asked of Him (1 John 5:14–15).

Chapter 7

A PLEA FOR A CLEAN HEART

Be gracious to me, O God, according to Your
lovingkindness....Wash me thoroughly from my iniquity and cleanse me from my sin....Purify me with
hyssop, and I shall be clean; wash me, and I shall be
whiter than snow....Create in me a clean heart, O
God, and renew a steadfast spirit within me.
—Psalm 51:1–2, 7, 10

N Psalm 51 we find one of David's most famous prayers.
It was written after the prophet Nathan confronted David
about his sin with Bathsheba, and in it David lays his heart
bare before God. He holds nothing back as he goes before the
Lord in repentance, and with each word it becomes clearer and
clearer why God called him a man after His own heart. David
wants only for their relationship to be restored. In this desperate plea David again shows us the types of prayers that will
draw us close to Father God's heart and align us with His will.

David begins by saying, "Be gracious to me, O God, according
to Your lovingkindness; according to the greatness of Your

compassion blot out my transgressions. Wash me thoroughly from my iniquity and cleanse me from my sin." Just the first line helps us understand a critical, fundamental truth. It lets us know we can ask God for grace. God's grace is an extension of His goodness toward us (Exod. 33:19; 34:6). We can ask God for His favor on our lives and be confident that He has a good will for us.

Many people struggle to believe that God really has a good will and a good purpose for their lives. They think that somehow God is withdrawn, angry, stoic, or judgmental. Oftentimes we get these wrong perceptions from our earthly parents or from the environment we grew up in. Ultimately, it is the power of darkness that has distorted our view of God. But by looking at David's prayer, we gain insight into the heart of God, and we see that God's disposition toward us is full of grace; it is good.

David was convinced of this. He said in Psalm 23, "Surely [Your] goodness and mercy shall follow me all the days of my life" (v. 6, KJV). He had confidence that God's purpose was to do him good. If you and I are going to have prayer lives that bring us freedom and deep connection with God, we must have confidence in who He is to us—that He is good and His plans for us are good.

David said, "Be gracious to me *according to Your lovingkindness.*" God is "abounding in lovingkindness and truth" (Exod. 34:6). Beloved, if you and I are going to walk with God, our belief about God and our prayer confession have to be in alignment with His nature, because our lives will not rise above our faith confession.

Our prayer life is a manifestation of who we believe God is, and when we begin to confess that God is good and gracious and has a heart of loving-kindness toward us, we're going to move deeper into the realms of eternal life and experience Him in a deeper way.

Father God is gracious in nature. He loves us and wants to do us good. The Lord is not up in the sky with a bat, angry and waiting to judge us. He sent His Son to die on the cross. The soldiers ripped out Messiah Jesus' beard. They whipped His back. They tore out His hair. They put a spear in His side. They nailed His hands and feet to the cross. Yet in the midst of this, Yeshua said, "Father, forgive them; for they do not know what they are doing" (Luke 23:34). And beyond this God's anger toward your sin was already taken out on Jesus. God is simply asking you now to come boldly before the throne of grace, confident in His love for you (Heb. 4:16). This is what David's prayer teaches us— that we can go boldly before the Lord, knowing He loves us and that His heart is to bless us.

Only He Can Satisfy

God's Word tells us that He "demonstrates His own love toward us, in that while we were yet sinners, Christ died for us" (Rom. 5:8). But oftentimes there's a block that keeps us from really believing this. I've read stories of men and women of God who were used mightily to impact the world with the gospel. Yet at the end of their lives, some of these servants of the Lord weren't fully convinced that God loved them.

I'd rather know that Jesus loves me than have the greatest impact on earth as a preacher. Yes, I want the Lord to use me to build His kingdom, but if I had to choose between having great impact on the earth as a preacher and simply knowing that God loves me, I would choose to simply know God loves me, because that's the only thing that satisfies.

Satisfaction comes only from relationship with Father God. Yeshua said, "This is eternal life, that they may know You, the only true God, and Jesus Christ whom You have sent" (John 17:3). True satisfaction is not found in becoming a great preacher, teacher, business leader, or whatever you think is going to make you somebody in the world's eyes. No; the way to find satisfaction is to know that God loves you. This is the confidence David had.

God created you because He wanted to have a relationship with you. He sent His Son to die for you because He loves you. And when Messiah Jesus died for you, He didn't die just to save you from hell. He didn't die just to forgive you of your sins. He died to marry you. You see, the Bible ends with what Scripture calls the marriage supper of the Lamb: "'Let us rejoice and be glad and give the glory to Him, for the marriage of the Lamb has come and His bride has made herself ready.' It was given to her to clothe herself in fine linen, bright and clean; for the fine linen is the righteous acts of the saints....'Blessed are those who are invited to the marriage supper of the Lamb.' And he said to me, 'These are true words of God'" (Rev. 19:7–9). We're called the bride of Christ. This is a divine picture of who we are to Him. God loves us personally, specifically, and uniquely. Jesus didn't die just for the world; He died for *you*. Yeshua said, "I chose you out of the world" (John 15:19).

Most of us have heard this scripture from Jeremiah: "For I know the plans that I have for you...plans for welfare and not for calamity to give you a future and a hope" (29:11). David knew God in this way. He had confidence in his future in God, and he didn't think God was far away. He believed the Lord was for him. He had confidence in God's goodwill and affection for him. So he said, "Lord, be gracious to me according to Your lovingkindness."

Cleansed From the Inside Out

After praying for God to be gracious to him, David began to pour out his heart to God, saying: "Wash me thoroughly from my iniquity and cleanse me from my sin....Purify me with hyssop, and I shall be clean; wash me, and I shall be whiter than snow....Create in me a clean heart, O God, and renew a steadfast spirit within me" (Ps. 51:2, 7, 10).

David had a deep desire to be washed of his sin. He wanted to be thoroughly cleansed of his iniquity so there would be nothing standing between him and Father God. David understood something that we must also embrace—that if we're not washed inside, we can't know God.

The Bible says, "Who may ascend into the hill of the Lord? And who may stand in His holy place? He who has clean hands and a pure heart" (Ps. 24:3–4). What God is saying here is that we can't walk in fellowship with Him unless our nature is purified. Yeshua said, "Blessed are the pure in heart, for they shall see God" (Matt. 5:8). In other words, if we are to walk closely with Messiah and become more like Him, we must be cleansed on the inside.

Beloved, we need to know our Creator is not far away somewhere up in the sky. He is here now in us. God has made known a glorious mystery, "which is Christ in you, the hope of glory" (Col. 1:27). Beloved, we aren't going to know Him in us and we're not going to know Him with us in a way that will bring us into deep satisfaction unless we are washed on the inside.

Forgiveness takes place in an instant. The moment we receive Jesus, we're legally forgiven. But to be washed is a process. The Bible says we are to be transformed by the renewing of our minds (Rom. 12:2). "But we all, with unveiled face, beholding as in a mirror the glory of the Lord, are being transformed into the same image from glory to glory, just as from the Lord, the Spirit" (2 Cor. 3:18). This is a process. It takes time and consistency to cleanse our hearts and minds of old ways.

"Create in me a clean heart; cleanse me from my sin; purify me with hyssop; wash me, and I shall be whiter than snow"— this type of prayer should be the cry of our hearts. This is deep calling to deep. As we're washed and cleansed and as His clean heart is created within us, we're brought into deep intimacy with Messiah Jesus. And deep intimacy with Yeshua is something that will satisfy us.

External and material things can never satisfy. Yeshua said, "One's life does not consist in the abundance of the things he possesses" (Luke 12:15, NKJV). The only thing that will bring us satisfaction is when we become more like Jesus, and as we do, we will know Him. Eternal life is, again, all about relationship.

Choose to Be Washed

David cried, "Lord, create in me a clean heart. Wash me thoroughly from my iniquity and cleanse me." Beloved, God cleanses us when we're willing to allow Him to cleanse us. In other words, we have to cooperate with God's sanctifying process. We have to become aware of what we're thinking and saying and be in a constant state of self-examination.

You see, we must choose whether we're going to let God shine His spotlight upon our lives. Many people run from the conviction of the Holy Spirit, but the Bible says, "The kindness of God leads you to repentance" (Rom. 2:4). The conviction of the Holy Spirit is God's kindness, causing us to become aware of our sins so we can look to Him and say, "Wash me, cleanse me, and give me a clean heart. I see that there is fear and evil in my heart [Rev. 21:8]. I see selfish ambition in my heart. I see pride in my heart. I see jealousy in my heart. O God, I know it's wrong. Forgive me. Wash me. Cleanse me." This is a prayer that when prayed from the heart will be answered.

It is so critical that we choose to be washed, to be regenerated, to be renewed. To David this was of the essence. In verse 6 David cried, "Behold, You desire truth in the innermost being, and in the hidden part You will make me know wisdom." David wanted God so desperately that he placed himself in a position to be examined by the Holy Spirit. He wanted the Lord to search him and find any impure way within him (Ps. 139:23–24). And if anything was found, his prayer was, "Lord, forgive me and put Your truth and wisdom in me."

When we put ourselves in this posture, our Creator is faithful to forgive us and to cleanse us from all unrighteousness (1 John 1:9). When we choose to let the Spirit of God in, we will be changed and transformed from the inside out. As we are, we will be taken into deeper depths in Yeshua—and as a result be filled with strength and joy.

After David asked God to cleanse him, he said, "Make me to hear joy and gladness, let the bones which You have broken rejoice" (v. 8). You see, as we hunger for God, as we cooperate with Him and ask Him to cleanse us, as we willingly repent, joy breaks forth in us. Yeshua's goodness is released from our innermost being. Messiah Yeshua said, "He who believes in Me, as the Scripture said, 'From his innermost being will flow rivers of living water'" (John 7:38). Beloved, everything we pray about is important, but the most important things are the deep issues of the heart. These are the prayer requests that get God's attention.

We All Need to Be Purified

In Psalm 51 David was calling out for restoration and cleansing from the sin he committed with Bathsheba. But I want you to know that all of us need to be washed and cleansed. We've all lost the innocence we had as children. As we age and move through life, the world has an effect on us. We are defiled by the fallen world we live in but even more so by the words we've spoken.

Jesus said, "It is not what enters into the mouth that defiles the man, but what proceeds out of the mouth, this defiles the man" (Matt. 15:11). When the Pharisees began to question Jesus as to why His disciples ate with unwashed hands, Jesus said, "There is nothing outside the man which can defile him if it goes into him; but the things which proceed out of the man are what defile the man" (Mark 7:15). In other words, eating food with unwashed hands does not defile a person. What defile people are the evil words that come out of their mouths.

It's no use hiding from God. He already knows everything in our hearts and every word we've ever said—all the critical, judgmental, and mean words we've spoken. We speak them because of an evil heart. Jesus said, "Out of the abundance of the heart his mouth speaks" (Luke 6:45, NKJV). Whether we want to admit it or not, you and I are defiled, and we need to get down on our knees and, like David, say, "Wash me and cleanse me, God, for You desire truth in the innermost being."

We cannot walk with God unless we're walking in truth. We can sit in all the church services we want to, but if we're leaving the services and speaking words of criticism, cruelty, and accusation against other people, these things defile us and our religion is a sham.

When Isaiah found himself in the presence of God, the prophet fell on his face before the Lord and said, "Woe is me, for I am ruined! Because I am a man of unclean lips, and I live among a people of unclean lips" (Isa. 6:5). Then he looked to Father God to wash and cleanse him, just as David did. The Lord graciously responded to Isaiah's plea by sending an angel to touch his mouth with a burning coal from the altar of God, and Isaiah's iniquity was taken away. In order to have peace in our hearts, in order to have restoration, in order for us to walk with God in a spirit of joy, we need to be washed and transformed. David realized this, so he cried, "Lord, cleanse me. Create in me a clean heart. Wash me with hyssop, and I shall be whiter than snow."

Dear one, I encourage you today to make a covenant before God to stop speaking evil. Choose to speak words of life instead of words of destruction. Choose to speak words that heal instead of words that tear people down. Life and death are in the power of the tongue, and our salvation experience will never rise above the confession of our mouth.

> For we all stumble in many ways. If anyone does not stumble in what he says, he is a perfect man, able to bridle the whole body as well. Now if we put the bits into the horses' mouths so that they will obey us, we direct their entire body as well. Look at the ships also, though

they are so great and are driven by strong winds, are still directed by a very small rudder wherever the inclination of the pilot desires. So also the tongue is a small part of the body, and yet it boasts of great things.

See how great a forest is set aflame by such a small fire! And the tongue is a fire, the very world of iniquity; the tongue is set among our members as that which defiles the entire body, and sets on fire the course of our life, and is set on fire by hell. For every species of beasts and birds, of reptiles and creatures of the sea, is tamed and has been tamed by the human race. But no one can tame the tongue; it is a restless evil and full of deadly poison. With it we bless our Lord and Father, and with it we curse men, who have been made in the likeness of God; from the same mouth come both blessing and cursing. My brethren, these things ought not to be this way.

—JAMES 3:2–10

So again, let's commit to guarding our hearts and watching what comes out of our mouths. Whenever a spirit of accusation, faultfinding, hostility, hatred, anger, or lust comes into our hearts, we must resist it. We can't always control every thought that comes into our minds or every impulse that strikes our hearts, but we can control what we do with those thoughts and impulses. We can either let them lodge in and speak them, or we can say, "Get behind me, Satan. Get out of my head."

If we're going to go deep with God, our words are going to have to line up with the Spirit of God. And we're going to have to be cleansed from the inside out. That is the only way we can walk with God, live in His presence, enjoy His fellowship, and experience the fullness of His blessing.

We're going to stand before the throne of Messiah, and He said we're going to give an account for every word that we speak (Matt. 12:36). So commit to speaking words that give life, words that heal, words that express faith and hope. Ask God to wash you with His Word and purify your heart. Ask Him to cleanse you of wrong thoughts about His love. If you and I want to truly walk with God and experience the joys that true faith produces, we need to pray as David did. "Wash me thoroughly from my iniquity and cleanse me from my sin....Create in me a clean heart, O God, and renew a steadfast spirit within me" (Ps. 51:2, 10).

Chapter 8

A PRAYER FOR GOD TO PROVE HIMSELF

At the time of the offering of the evening sacrifice, Elijah
the prophet came near and said, "O LORD, the God of
Abraham, Isaac and Israel, today let it be known that You
are God in Israel and that I am Your servant and I have
done all these things at Your word. Answer me, O LORD,
answer me, that this people may know that You, O LORD,
are God, and that You have turned their heart back again."
—1 KINGS 18:36–37

ELIJAH IS ONE of the best-known figures in the Hebrew
Bible. The New Testament tells us that Elijah was a man
just like you and me. Yet when he prayed that it would
not rain, it did not rain for three and a half years (Jas. 5:17).

The Book of Malachi prophesies that Elijah would announce
the coming of the Messiah (Mal. 4:5–6). In fact, when Jesus was
on earth, some skeptics asked Him, "Isn't Elijah supposed to come
first?" (See Mark 9:11.) Jesus answered, "Elijah has indeed come,

and they did to him whatever they wished, just as it is written of him" (Mark 9:12–13). He was referring to John the Baptist, whom Scripture says came as "a forerunner before [Yeshua] in the spirit and power of Elijah, to turn the hearts of the fathers back to the children, and the disobedient to the attitude of the righteous, so as to make ready a people prepared for the Lord" (Luke 1:17).

Elijah was a powerful, charismatic voice, unlike any other prophet in the Old Testament. Moses and Elijah appeared with Jesus on the Mount of Transfiguration as the two primary figures of the Old Testament, representing the Law and the prophets. Scripture tells of Elijah's many miracles and the outstanding way he displayed the glory of God. But among the best known of those exploits is Elijah's confrontation with the prophets of Baal on Mount Carmel. This is when he prayed:

> O LORD, the God of Abraham, Isaac and Israel, today let it be known that You are God in Israel and that I am Your servant and I have done all these things at Your word. Answer me, O LORD, answer me, that this people may know that You, O LORD, are God, and that You have turned their heart back again.
>
> —1 KINGS 18:36–37

If you think about the essence of this prayer, Elijah is asking, first, that God would prove Himself and show the prophets of Baal and the people of Israel that the Lord God of Israel is indeed the true God. Second, Elijah was asking God to vindicate him as His servant and show that he was acting at the command of the Lord.

Can you relate? Do family members, friends, neighbors, or people in your workplace refuse to believe Yeshua HaMashiach,

Jesus the Messiah, is truly the Lord? Do they instead not believe in God at all? Or do they believe in new age spirituality or some other religion? Perhaps they even make fun of you and treat you cynically and condescendingly. This is what Elijah the prophet was up against when he uttered this prayer.

The prophets of Baal believed their god was supreme. They laughed at Elijah and scorned the God of Israel. So the great prophet Elijah prayed to the Lord of heaven and said, "O God, prove to everybody that You are God." And the Lord answered in a dramatic way. As we examine this well-known prayer, we will discover an incredible promise that is available to us as God's people still today. But first, we must understand the context.

Calling Down God's Fire

During Elijah's day Israel had been led by a series of rulers who did evil in the sight of the Lord. Then Ahab came along, and he "did more to provoke the LORD God of Israel than all the kings of Israel who were before him" (1 Kings 16:33). Ahab married a wicked woman named Jezebel and led Israel to serve the god she worshipped, Baal. He even built a house and an altar to Baal, and his wife had the prophets of God killed.

This is when Elijah came on the scene. Scripture says, "Now Elijah the Tishbite, who was of the settlers of Gilead, said to Ahab, 'As the LORD, the God of Israel lives, before whom I stand, surely there shall be neither dew nor rain these years, except by my word'" (1 Kings 17:1).

At a time when the whole land seemed to have abandoned God and was following Baal, a man comes forward whose very name means "my God is Yahweh."[1] By declaring that there would be no rain until he said so, Elijah was essentially telling

Ahab that the God of Israel was greater than the god he worshipped. Baal was believed to be the god of fertility, the rain, the sun, and the storm. In other words, Baal was supposed to be lord of the weather, yet there would be no rain until God's prophet, not Baal, said so.

This made Ahab angry, and he sought to kill Elijah, sending out search parties to kingdoms far and wide. Elijah went into hiding for three years; then, when God told him it was time, Elijah arranged to meet with Ahab, and that is where he set up a spiritual showdown. "Now then send and gather to me all Israel at Mount Carmel," Elijah said, "together with 450 prophets of Baal and 400 prophets of the Asherah, who eat at Jezebel's table" (1 Kings 18:19).

Ahab couldn't back down from Elijah's challenge. He sent a message throughout Israel calling all the prophets of Baal to Mount Carmel. There they faced Elijah. You may know the rest of the story. Elijah prepared a sacrifice, as did the prophets of Baal. The prophets of Baal stacked up wood on the altar, and they called upon Baal to come down and consume the sacrifice. They cried and cried. They tore their clothes. They cut themselves. They screamed and shouted, but no fire fell from heaven.

Elijah began to make fun of them. He said, "Where's your God? Can he not hear? Where's Baal? Maybe he's taking a nap."

Finally, Elijah said enough is enough. To up the stakes, he had four pitchers of water poured over the wood on the altar. He had this done a second time, then a third time until the wood was drenched and the trench built around the altar was filled with water. Then Elijah called out to the God of Israel.

At the time of the offering of the evening sacrifice, Elijah the prophet came near and said, "O LORD, the God of Abraham, Isaac and Israel, today let it be known that You are God in Israel and that I am Your servant and I have done all these things at Your word. Answer me, O LORD, answer me, that this people may know that You, O LORD, are God, and that You have turned their heart back again." Then the fire of the LORD fell and consumed the burnt offering and the wood and the stones and the dust, and licked up the water that was in the trench. When all the people saw it, they fell on their faces; and they said, "The LORD, He is God; the LORD, He is God."

—1 KINGS 18:36–39

When Elijah cried out to the God of Israel, the fire fell, the sacrifice was consumed, and the wood was burned up. The fire even caused all the water to evaporate so there was nothing left but the smoke of the glory of God. Then Elijah commanded his servants to destroy the false prophets of Baal so that not one of them would escape.

Can you imagine seeing such an incredible display of God's power? My wife and I have been to Israel and visited Mount Carmel. What an unbelievable experience. This isn't some nice story told to make a point. The showdown at the mount really happened. Elijah saw God prove Himself in a supernatural way.

Beloved, you too can pray as Elijah prayed: "My Father God, please prove Yourself." Are there people in your life who believe in a false god or, again, who don't believe in God at all? Are there people in your life who are mocking Jesus and you? Beloved, you can say, "God, manifest Your glory and power."

Isn't that what Elijah was doing? Elijah said: "O Lord, God of

Abraham, Isaac, and Israel, today let it be known that You are God in Israel and that I am Your servant and I have done all these things at Your word."

I believe God wants to vindicate His children. You may be in a relationship and in some way the devil seems to have the upper hand. Perhaps you are facing some difficult dynamics with parents, in-laws, employers, or neighbors. You began to witness for Jesus or stand up for biblical morality and as a result have been marginalized. They began to twist your words or somehow made you feel small.

Whatever the reason, you began to pull back. You began to feel intimidated, and now you feel you have the lesser hand in that relationship, that Jesus isn't being magnified through your life as Lord. I want you to call upon Jesus and ask Him to prove that He's God in that relationship.

Ask Jesus to let His fire and glory fall. Whether the issue is between you and a brother or sister, your mom or dad, or a neighbor or coworker, I encourage you right now to get on your knees and do what Elijah did. Say, "O God, I love You. Jesus, I love You. I feel the devil right now is making fun of your Word, of Your truth, of Your salvation, and I ask You to send Your fire right now, Father God, and prove that You are God."

That is what Elijah prayed, and when he did, God's manifest presence fell, and God separated the true from the false. He set apart Elijah as His prophet, and He put to shame the prophets of Baal. I believe God wants to do that for His people still today. I believe He wants to do that for you. I believe God wants to bring a division in relationships that are causing dishonor to come upon Messiah Jesus.

You see, Yeshua said, "I did not come to bring peace, but a sword.

For I came to set a man against his father, and a daughter against her mother, and a daughter-in-law against her mother-in-law; and a man's enemies will be the members of his household" (Matt. 10:34–36). We have to be more concerned with standing with Jesus than with getting along with flesh and blood. Sometimes if you're going to inherit everything that Jesus has for you and if God's going to be able to do for you as much as He wants to do, you're going to have to make a decision to stand with Him, even if it alienates certain people that you're in relationship with right now. Elijah's relationship with Yahweh, the God of Israel, put him at odds with his culture and most of those who surrounded him.

I believe God wants to bring a separation in relationships in which you are unequally yoked with someone who is ungodly and continually makes fun of your relationship with Messiah. Beloved, the Lord wants to prove Himself to you and to me (Mal. 3:10), so don't be afraid to stand with Him, even if it means losing some relationships.

Ask Father God to cause His glory to fall in your life, just as it fell on Mount Carmel. Ask Father God to prove Himself on earth within your sphere of influence. When Jesus walked on earth, He always was in control. Even when He went to the cross, He was in control. He was able to silence the Pharisees and Sadducees, and the Lord backed up His word with miracles, signs, and wonders. God has proved Himself over and over again, so ask Him to do it again.

Walk in Wisdom

I must stress, however, that some of us may be walking in situations in life where people are not receiving our witness, and it may not be just because of God's glory not being manifest. It may be because we've been walking unwisely. If we haven't been walking in wisdom, then we're going to have a difficult time getting people to listen to us. Sometimes we keep casting our pearls before swine. This is unwise, and it doesn't help. Messiah Yeshua said, "Do not give what is holy to dogs, and do not throw your pearls before swine, or they will trample them under their feet, and turn and tear you to pieces" (Matt. 7:6).

Also, if you believe you've been walking in stubbornness and pride, which have been keeping people from receiving your witness, I encourage you to repent right now. If your own behavior has been in the way of the glory of God being manifest in your relationship so that He can be proved to your sphere of influence, ask the Lord to forgive you, and then know that it's done.

Right now I speak increase over you. I declare, in the name of Jesus, that you're going to walk in wisdom from this point forward, and you're going to walk in such a way that the people around you will have to take notice of the supernatural wisdom that's on your life.

Beloved, the same God who answered Elijah on Mount Carmel is alive and well today. He will prove Himself when we call on Him. He will show a world that is turning its back on Him and His ways that "the LORD, He is God." So just ask Him to do it. Ask Him to cause you to live as a light in this world so that even your enemies will be forced to admit to themselves that the glory of God is on your life. Our God is God, and if you ask Him, He will prove Himself to you.

The Holy Spirit is our portion, and we can live in victory

in this world, displaying God's glory and supremacy to all those around us, even to those who don't like us and reject us. I declare right now in the name of Jesus that by God's Spirit you're going to walk in a higher realm of supernatural glory than you've ever walked in before, proving to the world that the Lord is God, just as Elijah did.

Despite everything I've said, I want to make room for the fact that with the Lord a day is like a thousand years to us, and sometimes things are not made right immediately. That's why Jesus said many who will be last will be first and many who will be first will be last. Sometimes God's glory will not fall upon injustice and idolatry until the end of the age, but we should still pray for God's glory to fall, for Him to destroy evil, and for Him to be exalted in and through our lives so people will recognize His goodness, glory, and power in us.

That is why Jesus said the Father's will for our lives is that people would see His goodness upon us and look up and give Him glory. It's that we would be like lights on a hill. So I want to encourage you to keep praying even when injustice and mountains that need to be moved have not moved yet. One thing I know for sure is that God wants to prove Himself to you, whether your external reality is brought fully into balance right now or not. Because of God's eternal perspective, we can't guarantee when it will happen, but one thing we should believe and contend for is that we will know Yeshua's victory in and through our lives and that we will walk in such power that our presence will penetrate people undeniably, even if they won't admit it.

Jesus walked in this type of power. When the soldiers arrived to arrest Him and asked Yeshua if He was Jesus of Nazareth, Yeshua said, "I am," and they all fell to the ground. (See John

18:1–6.) They still arrested Him, but the glory of God was undeniable. So I speak over you increase so that you will walk continually in an ever-increasing way in the resurrection, power, and glory of God. Whether people recognize it or not, I pray that it will be real to you and that you will live in that glory and experience His victory.

Sometimes bad things happen to good people, but that doesn't mean you will lose your victory in the process. If our victory is dependent on circumstances, we'll never have victory. Stephen was stoned to death with a smile on his face. Those around him said he looked like an angel. He saw Jesus as he was being stoned, and he experienced God's glory in the process (Acts 7:54–60). Stephen's circumstances didn't determine whether he had victory. He had victory because he knew Yeshua, and Yeshua proved Himself to Stephen even in the midst of the chaos. I believe that as you earnestly seek God's face first in your life, He will do the same for you.

Chapter 9

SEEKING SPIRITUAL SIGHT

Then Elisha prayed and said, "O LORD, I pray, open his
eyes that he may see." And the LORD opened the servant's eyes and he saw; and behold, the mountain was
full of horses and chariots of fire all around Elisha.
—2 KINGS 6:17

WHO ISN'T IMPRESSED by Elijah's great and mighty
works, but did you know Elisha performed even
more miracles than Elijah did?

Elisha is a fascinating figure. He was Elijah's servant, and
he followed Elijah everywhere he went. Elisha's whole ministry
was serving the prophet Elijah. Then, at the end of Elijah's life,
Elisha asked to receive a double portion of the anointing that
was on Elijah, and that is exactly what happened. The anointing
that fell upon Elisha was even stronger than the one Elijah carried, and he worked twice as many miracles as Elijah did.

It's hard to imagine. What was it about Elisha that caused
him to receive a double portion of such a powerful anointing?

Receiving a Greater Anointing

First, Elisha recognized the anointing that was on Elijah. You see, the anointing you respect is the anointing you will receive from. Elisha was able to receive the anointing that was on Elijah because he recognized the anointing that was on Elijah and he submitted to it. In today's culture people have so much pride and have been so brainwashed by the spirit of fear that they have a hard time submitting to others.

Sometimes we miss what we could have absorbed from someone who is walking in a higher level than we are because we have too much pride to get into right alignment with that person. This applies not just to the spiritual realm but even to the earthly realm. For instance, if we work for someone who has a great business mind, we aren't going to receive from that person by arguing with him or her. No; we must place ourselves in a position of subjection to learn from the person and receive what God has placed inside that individual.

So many of us lose opportunities to glean from others because of rebellion and pride. We often lack humility because of feelings of inferiority and self-defensiveness, so we resist being in a posture through which we can receive from the one who is more advanced. This makes life so much more difficult than it ever needed to be. Elisha recognized the anointing that was on Elijah; thus, he was able to receive from it. He didn't have to start his ministry from scratch; he started from Elijah's shoulders.

Second, because Elisha recognized the anointing that was on Elijah's life, he stayed close to him. For instance, if you are involved in a ministry and recognize an anointing on your pastor or someone else in the congregation, do you know what you should do? You should stay as close to that person as common sense in the Lord will allow, because the more time you spend with that person, the more you're going to absorb the anointing from that person.

You see, you can absorb an anointing through osmosis and through transfer. The person you are five years from now will be largely determined by the people you spend your time with during this period of time. If you spend your time with people who are more anointed, more advanced, and more knowledgeable than you are, in five years you're going to be so much more anointed, so much more advanced, and so much more knowledgeable than you would be if you were to spend the next five years with people who are at the same level as you are or a lower level. Anointings, knowledge, and spiritual power are transferable. We pick them up just by being in close proximity with people who are anointed, knowledgeable, and walking in the power of God.

This is just common sense. I had a desire to learn wilderness survival skills, so I spent time with wilderness survival experts. I picked up a little bit of what they have just by spending four days in the woods with them. I didn't avoid them; I went to them and spent time with them so that what is on them could be imparted to me. When I was with them, I didn't try to prove myself or argue with them. I didn't criticize them. Rather, I humbled myself and put myself in a posture where I could receive, absorb, and learn.

Elisha stayed very close to Elijah. Toward the end of Elijah's life, when Elijah announced that he was about to depart this world, Elisha cried out, "'Please, let a double portion of your spirit be upon me.' [Elijah] said, 'You have asked a hard thing.

Nevertheless, if you see me when I am taken from you, it shall be so for you; but if not, it shall not be so'" (2 Kings 2:9–10).

What was Elijah saying? He was telling Elisha, "You have to get focused on me and stay close to me so the anointing that's on me can come upon you. If you take your eyes off me, if you get distracted, then the anointing that's on me won't come upon you when I leave."

Elisha took Elijah at his word. He stayed focused. He stayed fixed. And when Elijah was taken away, Elisha saw him, and a double portion of Elijah's anointing came upon Elisha. And as a result, he did twice as many miracles as Elijah did.

That is why in the Hebrew Bible we learn that we should respect our elders. We do it to get their help. We respect our elders so the stability and wisdom that has been developed in them can come upon us. It's true in the natural, and it's true in the supernatural.

Beloved, if you know people who are anointed, guard yourself against the law of familiarity. You may have heard the expression that familiarity breeds contempt. We can become so used to somebody who is more anointed and advanced than we are that we begin to take the person for granted. Not only do we take them for granted; we even begin to dishonor them.

This happened to Jesus. When He went into His hometown, the people there said, "We know Your mom and dad. We know Joseph and Mary. Who do You think You are?" And the Bible says they became offended with Him. (See Mark 6:2–3.) Jesus responded by saying, "A prophet is not without honor except in his hometown and among his own relatives and in his own household" (Mark 6:4). Their familiarity with Jesus bred contempt.

So again, I want to admonish you to be careful not to take your pastor and spiritual leaders for granted. Don't stop being impacted by their messages. Don't stop taking advantage of the opportunities they give you for growth, whether it's taking classes or serving in an area of ministry. Be careful that you don't lose the opportunity to receive more of the anointing that's on them because, again, anointings are transferable.

That's why Paul told Timothy, "Do not neglect the spiritual gift within you, which was bestowed on you through prophetic utterance with the laying on of hands by the presbytery" (1 Tim. 4:14). Through the laying on of hands, a spiritual gift was imparted to Timothy.

After he received the anointing that had been on Elijah's life, Elisha did even more miracles than Elijah was able to do. He was able to receive the anointing by respecting, acknowledging, and honoring the anointing that was on Elijah, then staying close to him and focused on him. By doing this, the holy power of God that was on Elijah came upon Elisha even double-fold.

The same spiritual law can work for you today, beloved. Many great men and women of God became great because they stayed close to a spiritual mentor, spiritual father, or spiritual mother. As Elisha grew in the anointing on his life, he too became a mentor to others. In fact, Elisha's prayer in 2 Kings 6 wasn't for himself but for his servant.

To See Beyond the Natural

The prayer occurs in verses 15–18:

> Now when the attendant of the man of God had risen early and gone out, behold, an army with horses and chariots was circling the city. And his servant said to him, "Alas, my master! What shall we do?" So he answered,

"Do not fear, for those who are with us are more than those who are with them." Then Elisha prayed and said, "O LORD, I pray, open his eyes that he may see." And the LORD opened the servant's eyes and he saw; and behold, the mountain was full of horses and chariots of fire all around Elisha. When they came down to him, Elisha prayed to the LORD and said, "Strike this people with blindness, I pray." So He struck them with blindness according to the word of Elisha.

In this particular story, Israel was being attacked by the king of Aram, and it looked as though Israel was outnumbered. But what Elisha saw in the spirit realm was the supernatural hosts that were on Israel's side. Of course, Elisha's attendant couldn't see it. He was scared because he was seeing only in the natural. So what was Elisha's prayer? He said, "Lord, open my servant's eyes that he might be able to see in the spirit world and that he might understand that there are more for us than against us." Elisha's prayer, beloved one, was for spiritual sight.

We need to be able to see. We need to be able to see beyond the temporal. We need to be able to see through the material world. We need to see what is beyond what is happening this very second. We need to be able to see through the circumstances. We need to be able to see through what people say. We need to be able to see with the eyes of the Spirit. The Bible tells us that the things that are real are not the things that are seen because the things that are seen are passing away. Rather, the things that are real are the things that are unseen (2 Cor. 4:18). We need to see with the lens of eternity.

Do you have a desire to see in the spirit world? I know I do. One of my common themes in prayer is what Elisha asked for:

"Lord, open my eyes that I can see. Lord, I want to be able to see in the spirit." Our fight is not against flesh and blood, but it's against principalities and forces of spiritual wickedness in heavenly places (Eph. 6:10–18).

You see, we live in a spiritual world, and we're not going to be able to live in victory if we don't have spiritual sight. Jesus was able to see in the spirit. The Bible says He knew what was in the hearts of all men (John 2:24–25). He had wisdom and understanding. If you and I don't have spiritual sight, which is a supernatural gift given by the Spirit of Elohim, the Spirit of God, we are going to walk around floundering and fumbling in life. We're going to live at an earthly level. We're never going to soar on the heights to live in spiritual victory because to live in victory, we must see reality as it truly is, and the only way to do that is to see with the eyes of God's Spirit.

Paul prayed in the Book of Ephesians that God would open the eyes of our hearts (Eph. 1:18). Think about that. Paul prayed that God would open the eyes of our hearts and understanding. In order to see in the spirit, we have to be able to see and perceive what cannot be seen and perceived simply in the natural. Seeing in the spirit involves the supernatural ability to understand people, your circumstances, and the spirit world in which you live.

Now, this may sound way out there to some people, but I'm here to tell you this is not way out there. This is not pie in the sky. This is what it means to walk in supernatural revelation and wisdom, and we should be asking for it just as Elisha did. We must pray, "Lord, let me see. Let me have revelation."

Revelation gives sight. Jesus said to Peter, "'Who do you say that I am?' Simon Peter answered, 'You are the Christ, the Son of the living God.' And Jesus said to him, 'Blessed are you,

Simon Barjona, because flesh and blood did not reveal this to you, but My Father who is in heaven. I also say to you that you are Peter, and upon this rock I will build My church'" (Matt. 16:15–18).

What rock was Jesus referring to here? Part of the rock, beloved, is having revelation. The revelation Peter had allowed him to see that Jesus is the Son of God when others couldn't discern that. Peter had spiritual sight. That is my prayer for you, that you will have spiritual sight and that God will open your eyes to see in the spirit and perceive what cannot be perceived in the natural. My prayer is that you will walk in a spirit of wisdom and revelation in the Holy Spirit and that you will walk in the supernatural, because when you walk in the supernatural, you walk in victory.

༄༅

Elisha prayed for his servant's eyes to be opened. This is a prayer that God will answer, beloved. It is one that is more than a superficial request. It is God's desire for you. He wants you to see with spiritual eyes, walk in a greater anointing, and go from grace to grace and glory to glory.

Chapter 10

A PLEA FOR SUPERNATURAL INCREASE

> Now Jabez called on the God of Israel, saying, "Oh
> that You would bless me indeed and enlarge my
> border, and that Your hand might be with me, and
> that You would keep me from harm that it may not
> pain me!" And God granted him what he requested.
> —1 CHRONICLES 4:10

ONE OF MY favorite things about the prayer of Jabez is that it is so simple and childlike. We don't know much about Jabez's life and history, but we know that when he went before the Lord with a pure and sincere heart, praying for Father God to bless him and enlarge his territory, God answered. The good news for you and me, beloved, is that God's goodness toward us is the same as it was toward Jabez.

How do I know that? Scripture declares this repeatedly. Paul began his many letters to the early church by saying, "Grace to you and peace from God our Father and the Lord Jesus

Christ." (See Romans 1:7, 1 Corinthians 1:3, 2 Corinthians 1:2, Galatians 1:3, Ephesians 1:2, Philippians 1:2, Colossians 1:2, 1 Thessalonians 1:1, 2 Thessalonians 1:2, 1 Timothy 1:2, 2 Timothy, Titus 1:4, and Philemon 3.) This means God's favor is on you and me. It means that He loves us and when we ask Him for good things, as Jabez did, He's going to give them to us.

Jesus said, "If you then, being evil, know how to give good gifts to your children, how much more will your Father who is in heaven give what is good to those who ask Him!" (Matt. 7:11). You're not condemned before Father God. He's not mad at you. Your future isn't going to be filled with gloom and doom. The enemy wants us to believe his lies. But the truth is that God loves us, we are His children, and His desire is to bless us.

Knowing God as Father

The Bible says, "For you have not received a spirit of slavery leading to fear again, but you have received a spirit of adoption as sons by which we cry out, 'Abba! Father!'" (Rom. 8:15). Abba is a term that means daddy. Beloved, God is your Father. Do you realize that? When you pray, do you ever call God your daddy? Do you address Him as God, or do you address Him as Father, Abba, Daddy, or Papa? Some people, if they're honest, will tell you they never call God Father when they pray. Instead, they say God or Lord. Yes, the Lord is our God, but our God came to us in the person of Messiah Jesus so He could become our Father and we could know Him as Daddy. We've not received a spirit of isolationism; we've received the spirit of adoption by which we cry, "Daddy, Father."

I once read the story of a Muslim woman from Pakistan, who was raised to believe the Quran was the true word of God.

But during a very difficult time in her life, supernatural things started happening to her, and eventually someone put a Judeo-Christian Bible in her hands. This woman wasn't interested in the Bible at the time, but so many unexplainable, supernatural things began to happen to her that she picked it up one day.

Suddenly, as she began to read the Bible, it was like something became alive in her. Spiritual life began to spring forth. But she was terrified because she had been taught her whole life that the Quran is right and the Bible we have as Christians is incorrect. The Quran told her that Jesus isn't really the Son of God, that He didn't really die on the cross and ascend to heaven but that Muhammad is the highest prophet.

As she continued reading the Judeo-Christian Bible, she discovered that the writings of the Old and New Testaments contradicted the Quran and what she had been taught as a Muslim. She became very confused. Finally, in desperation she fell on her knees, held the Quran in one hand and the Bible in the other, and said, "God, which one is true?" Next, she shared, the Spirit of the Lord spoke to her and said, "Which one tells you to call Me Father?" That totally melted her heart. She put down her Islamic defenses toward Christianity and received Yeshua as her Lord. The revelation of God as a loving Father saved her life.

You see, the Quran never taught her to relate to God as Father. In the Quran, God was someone way up in the sky, too holy really to be approached or know. But in the Judeo-Christian Bible, Jesus said, "Pray, then, in this way: '*Our Father* who is in heaven, hallowed be Your name'" (Matt. 6:9, emphasis added).

As we study the prayer of Jabez, I want you to realize that we're praying to someone who is a Father to us and loves us as

His children, someone who has good things in store for us and wants to bless us by bringing good things into our lives.

Trusting the God of Israel

Jabez is mentioned only briefly in Scripture, but his prayer is filled with revelation that applies just as much to us today as it did to him. Let's examine his prayer line by line.

> Now Jabez called on the God of Israel, saying, "Oh that You would bless me indeed and enlarge my border, and that Your hand might be with me, and that You would keep me from harm that it may not pain me!" And God granted him what he requested.
>
> —1 CHRONICLES 4:10

First, notice that "Jabez called on the God of Israel." Our faith is a Judeo-Christian faith. As a Christian you too serve the God of Israel because He is the Father of Messiah Jesus. That's why it is important for us to know our God, not only through the New Testament but also through the pages of the Old. Knowing God's revelation through the Old Testament is the only way we can have a complete and full understanding of our faith. That is why Yeshua said to the Samaritan woman in John 4, "Salvation is from the Jews" (v. 22). Jabez's prayer was to the God of Israel, the God and Father of the Lord Jesus Christ, who is also your God.

Next, we see that Jabez prayed, "Oh that You would bless me indeed." I just love that. Jabez didn't just want to be blessed; he wanted to be blessed indeed. He wanted God to bless his socks off. Beloved, we have a big God. Let's believe Him for big things. Let's not believe Him for just a little. Let's believe Him for a whole lot.

Shortly before his death, the prophet Elisha told the king of

Israel to take an arrow and strike the ground as a declaration of victory over his enemy, the Arameans. The king struck the ground three times and then stopped. Elisha was angry with the king and said, "You should have struck five or six times, then you would have struck Aram until you would have destroyed it. But now you shall strike Aram only three times" (2 Kings 13:19). The king could have won a complete and absolute victory, but because he only had a vision for a partial victory, that's all he received.

When Yeshua healed two blind men, He told them, "It shall be done to you according to your faith" (Matt. 9:29). The same is true for you and me. Father God responds to our faith. So I want to encourage you to not just believe God to bless you and not just ask God to bless you but ask Him to triply bless you. Ask Him to do what Jabez asked Him to do—bless you indeed. Ask Him to bring blessing upon blessing upon blessing on your life and cause you to bring glory to His name by living in that blessing.

There Is More!

Jabez goes on to say, "Lord, that You would bless me indeed and enlarge my border." Beloved, the Lord doesn't want us to stay where we are. Father God wants to bring you and me into a fuller and bigger place in the Spirit. He wants more for us because He is a God of more. There's always more in God. There are always higher heights and deeper depths in Him, and it's going to be like this forever.

Jabez's prayer was, "Lord, enlarge my border. Bring me into a fuller experience of You. Bring me into a fuller peace. Bring me into a fuller victory. Bring me into a fuller joy. Bring me into a fuller happiness." I want you to know that there is more for you and me in Messiah Jesus. If you and I don't believe that, then something's wrong. Our God is continuously, effervescently, effortlessly, eternally bubbling up more. He's always new. He's always fresh. He's always more.

That's why the angels in Revelation 4 don't cease crying out day and night, "Holy, holy, holy." They say this forever and ever because every time they say, "Holy," they're responding to a new revelation of the glory of God. Every time they say, "Holy," it's like a fresh wave of who God is rolls over them. Every time they say, "Holy," it's like their breath has been taken away. With every "Holy, holy, holy" they say, they are being continually overwhelmed with a new wave of God's goodness and glory.

God has more for you and me. He wants to enlarge our borders and bring us into a deeper realm of *shalom*, a deeper experience of fullness in the Holy Spirit, a deeper place of knowing Father God. Beloved, there's more for you. Keep asking and keep seeking, because as you continue to ask, as you continue to seek, and as you continue to knock, God's going to bring you into more. That's what makes living for Messiah Jesus exciting. It's a walk of discovery, a discovery of the more.

After Jabez prayed, "Enlarge my border," he said, "And that Your hand might be with me." He was praying, "Father, *wherever I go*, let Your hand be with me." Jabez was yearning for a supernatural consciousness of God's favor on his life. He was asking, "Lord, put Your hand on me. Be with me. Give me favor and open up the way for me wherever I go."

Remember Jacob? Wherever he went, his flock multiplied (Gen. 30:25–43). Jacob was blessed everywhere he went because God was with him *everywhere he went*. Not only that. Whoever was with Jacob was blessed just because they were with him. I believe that's what God wants for you and me. He wants to bless us indeed, just as Jabez prayed, and He wants everybody who is connected to us to be blessed and better off for having been in relationship with us.

I know that's my desire. I want all my staff to be blessed because of their relationship with me and this ministry. That's what God wants for all of us too. He blesses us to make us a blessing.

Secure in Him

Finally, Jabez prayed, "Oh that You would bless me indeed and enlarge my border, and that Your hand might be with me, and *that You would keep me from harm that it may not pain me!*" There are so many dangers all around us in the world, and these are not pretend dangers. But those who know God can have the assurance that they're safe and secure, even in this dangerous world.

Psalm 91 is a beautiful example of this. In this psalm we read: "He who dwells in the shelter of the Most High will abide in the shadow of the Almighty....A thousand may fall at your side and ten thousand at your right hand, but it shall not approach you....For you have made the LORD, my refuge, even the Most High, your dwelling place. No evil will befall you, nor will any plague come near your tent" (Ps. 91:1, 7, 9–10).

Years ago I was struggling in life, and I was seeing all these dangers around me. I was seeing so many of God's children just failing and getting hurt, and I was so grieved by it. I said, "God, what can I do? I want to trust You and I want to believe You, but it seems like so many who say they know Jesus are not being protected." And the Lord spoke to me and said, "The reason You're seeing what You're seeing is because My people are not trusting Me and clinging to Me." In other words, they're not abiding under the shelter and the shadow of the Most High God. They're out there on their own, not depending on God but living independently of Him, even though they call themselves Christians.

Around this time, the Lord gave me the assurance that I could trust Him to make Psalm 91 a reality in my life. I was in my office, and my Bible was in the sanctuary under a chair, and I said, "Lord, if I can really believe that You'll do for me what Psalm 91 says You'll do—that You're going to keep me safe under Your protection and that even if a thousand fall at my side and ten thousand at my right hand, no evil is going to befall me—if I can really believe You for that, then I'm going to go out to where my Bible is and pick it up, and if it just randomly opens to Psalm 91, then I'll know I can trust You to do for me what Psalm 91 says You'll do." Sometimes God calls us to put down a fleece, as Gideon did, and that's what I was doing here.

After saying that to God, I walked into the sanctuary, took my Bible out from under the chair where it was sitting, and just randomly opened it up. Where did it fall open to? Exactly to Psalm 91. Beloved, what Father did, is doing, and will do for me is exactly what He'll do for all His children as we trust Him and cling to Him, not living in our flesh, independent of our Creator, but living dependent on Him.

——

What God did for Jabez He'll do for you. But hear me: we must ask Him. Jabez asked. Beloved, I encourage you to ask God to bless you. Ask God to enlarge your territory, to bring you into a fuller place in His Spirit, where you'll experience more joy, more love, more *shalom*, and more dominion in the Spirit. Ask God to be with you where you go as you depend on Him, giving you favor and opening up the way for you. Ask God to keep you from harm and from unnecessary pain through His divine protection on your life. As you look to Him in love, He's going to do it.

Chapter 11

LOOKING TO GOD FOR SOMETHING NEW

Thus says the LORD who made the earth, the LORD
who formed it to establish it, the LORD is His name,
"Call to Me and I will answer you, and I will tell you
great and mighty things, which you do not know."
—JEREMIAH 33:2–3

To ME, JEREMIAH 33:3 is one of the most exciting verses in the Hebrew Bible. I especially love the way it reads in the King James Version: "Call unto me, and I will answer thee, and show thee great and mighty things, which thou knowest not." The idea is that if we call upon our Creator to show us things that we're not able to perceive in the natural, the Lord is going to open up mysteries so we can see what we can't see in the natural, go where we couldn't go in the natural, and experience what we can never experience in the natural world.

I don't know about you, but that excites me. Do you remember what it was like when you were a child and everything was new?

You had a great sense of adventure. Going to new places and experiencing things for the first time was wondrous. Life was an adventure as you experienced things for the first time. But as we age, the adventure of life begins to diminish. It becomes more and more like, "I've been there and I've done that." The things that once captured our hearts become blasé.

For example, when I was a young person, I used to go searching for frogs and snakes. I remember exploring and feeling as if I was one with nature. Every summer for me was like a brand-new experience. But as I aged, I had experienced some of those things so many times that some of the wonder began to wear off. How do we get back that sense of wonder? How do we get back that sense of fascination? We go beyond the natural into the supernatural because in the supernatural life is always new.

That's what I love so much about these verses in Jeremiah 33. The Lord said, "Call upon Me and I will show you great and wondrous things, marvelous things, fascinating things, things that you've not seen or heard before and that you know not of." In the supernatural, life is always new, and we're always experiencing new things. There's always a sense of wonder and adventure. Not that we necessarily feel it every second, but it's real. So I can go to Papa God in the morning, call out to Him, and say, "Lord, show me something marvelous. Show me something new. Reveal something to me that will fascinate me; make my life an adventure," because in the Spirit there is always something more, always something new, always something exciting.

There are only two places in the entire Word of God where we find a threefold repetition of any of God's attributes. We find many of God's characteristics throughout the Bible but not repeated three times in a row. We know, for example, that God is what we call omnipotent; He's all-powerful. But nowhere in the Bible do we hear repeated three times in a row that God is omnipotent, omnipotent, and omnipotent.

We know that God is loving. But nowhere in the Bible do we see God referred to as all loving, all loving, all loving. Nowhere do we see Him referred to as faithful, faithful, faithful, although we know He is faithful. Again, there are only two times in the Bible when we see a threefold repetition of any of God's attributes: in Isaiah 6 and Revelation 4. Isaiah and John actually get a glimpse into the heavens and see the Lord high and lifted up upon His throne. As they see the Lord upon the throne, they hear the angels crying out day and night, "*Holy, holy, holy* is the LORD God, the Almighty, who was and who is and who is to come" (Rev. 4:8, emphasis added; see also Isaiah 6:3).

Now, I want you to consider this for a moment: if you just heard someone in the natural saying the same word over and over again, it would become monotonous. But that's not what is happening in Isaiah 6 and Revelation 4. What is happening is that the glory and presence of God are continuing to be manifest in greater and greater wonders, in a higher and more glorious fashion so that each time a new wave of God's glory is released, the angels are so overwhelmed and taken aback that they respond by saying, "Holy."

I discussed this briefly in the previous chapter, but I want to explore this further. God is effervescently alive, and there is always something new bubbling up from Him. Every time a new revelation of who God is bubbles up from within Him— each time a new wave of glory emanates from the Father, the Son, and the Spirit—the angels say, "Holy," so they are continually saying, "Holy, holy, holy." They're continually overwhelmed by each new manifestation of the wonder of God. It's always fresh, and it's always new.

So when the Lord tells us in Jeremiah 33:3, "Call unto me, and I will answer thee, and show thee great and mighty things, which thou knowest not" (KJV), what this means is that you and I can continue to be fascinated with life and captured by adventure and wonder as we move forward into the depths of eternal life. It means God continues to give us fresh revelation of who He is. That is why living for Messiah Yeshua is so exciting.

I want to be fascinated with God. And do you know what? If our relationship with God is real, if it's vital, God is always going to be doing something fresh and new in our lives. Now, I will grant that it doesn't seem, at least for me personally, that there's a new revelation or something new every day. But I view this as seasons. God is continually bringing me into fresh seasons of revelation. He is continually doing fresh things in my life, even though some days I have to just keep putting one foot in front of the other, putting one sock on at a time and walking it out, just practicing what He has already shown me to practice and being obedient to what He has asked me to do.

There are many days when it seems as if nothing is new. But overall, if we take a step back, we'll be able to see that God is continually bringing us into a new thing—if we're really pursuing Him. God wants to continually bring something new and fresh into our lives.

Stay Fascinated

Maybe you're at a place in your life where you're feeling stagnant. Maybe you're at a place in life where you just feel that nothing is new anymore. Nothing excites you anymore, and you're having a hard time staying motivated. Call unto the Lord. Ask Father God to show and tell you great and wonderful things that you know not of. We can trust God to do what He said He would do.

In Yeshua HaMashiach, old things pass away and all things become new. You and I are new creations in Christ Jesus (2 Cor. 5:17). Our God is alive. He is always new, and He has given us eternal life. Life is always new.

If you're feeling stuck, I speak freshness over you right now in Messiah Jesus' name. I declare over your life something new in the Holy Spirit. I pray you will open your heart and allow Father God to fascinate you with the wonders of His presence. I pray that He will recapture your heart, ignite in you a passion for Him, and push you deeper into the realm of eternal life. The Lord wants to irresistibly draw you and me.

I've said this before, but it bears repeating. Yeshua said, "Seek and ye shall find. Knock, and the door will be opened. Ask, and you'll receive." (See Matthew 7:7–8.) In the Greek, the language in which the New Testament Scriptures were given to us, the verb tense is saying, "Keep asking; keep seeking; keep knocking." In other words, don't just do it one time; press in for more. Keep asking; keep seeking; keep knocking. And as you keep asking and keep seeking and keep knocking, God is going to release to you a fresh flow of His Spirit, and there will be continual momentum and power in your life.

Chaverim ("friends" in Hebrew), some of us say we desire God, but if we really desire Him, we're going to do something about it. If we're really thirsty for God, we're going to call out to Him and pray. We're going to ask. We're going to seek. We're going to knock. We're going to repent of sin. We're going to fast by denying ourselves things in the natural so we can receive more of the supernatural. If your desire for God's living water is so intense that you're actually taking action to seek Him, He's going to do something new for you.

The Lord says, "Draw near to Me, and I will draw near to you. Seek Me and you will find Me. Call upon Me and I will tell thee great and marvelous things that thou knowest not of." (See James 4:8, Jeremiah 29:13, and Jeremiah 33:3.) So ask Him to release a new impartation of His glory into your life. Even as you sleep at night, Father God will minister new things to you. He will bring new people, circumstances, and revelation into your life that will reignite your passion for Him. He will take you to the next level so that you might continue your journey in Him and stay fascinated.

⤜⤜⤜⤜

God loves you, beloved, and He has much more for your life and mine than we realize. All we need to do is put Him first and pursue Him. I promise that as you do, your life is going to forever be new. I have a friend who is eighty-four years old, and she's like a teenager because she's so hungry for God. Father God is continually doing something new in her life, and she has been a believer for forty years.

Dear one, let's not be passive Christians. Let's not just sit around waiting for something to happen. If we really believe God the way we say we do, we're going to do something to seek Him. We're going to do something to lay hold of Him. We're going to draw near to Him. And as we do, He's going to draw near to us.

PART III

Paul the Apostle: The Domain of Power and Love

Chapter 12

A PRAYER FOR INSIGHT AND REVELATION

For this reason I...do not cease giving thanks for you, while making mention of you in my prayers; that the God of our Lord Jesus Christ, the Father of glory, may give to you a spirit of wisdom and of revelation in the knowledge of Him. I pray that the eyes of your heart may be enlightened, so that you will know what is the hope of His calling, what are the riches of the glory of His inheritance in the saints, and what is the surpassing greatness of His power toward us who believe.
—EPHESIANS 1:15–19

P AUL'S LETTER TO the Ephesians is unlike many of the other epistles he wrote to the early churches. Instead of pointing out problems in the congregation, though those existed, Paul spent time in Ephesians explaining core truths of the gospel and how to apply them to our lives.

In the first chapter, Paul wrote that we have been blessed

"with every spiritual blessing in the heavenly places in Christ" (v. 3) and that Father "chose us in Him [Jesus] before the foundation of the world" (v. 4), "predestined us to adoption as sons through Jesus Christ to Himself" (v. 5), and sealed us "in Him with the Holy Spirit of promise" (v. 13).

Then, near the end of Ephesians 1, Paul prayed for the body of Messiah—that is, you and me—that we would experience the reality of what Yeshua provided for us through His death on the cross. It is God's heart to give you and me, His children on earth today, the same things Paul was asking for two thousand years ago. So I want to walk you through this prayer because Paul's requests in Ephesians 1 reflect the Father's will for your life. And as you know by now, when we pray according to His will, He will answer.

Paul introduced his prayer by saying, "Having heard of the *faith* in the Lord Jesus which exists among you and your *love* for all the saints, [I] do not cease giving thanks for you, while making mention of you in my prayers" (vv. 15–16, emphasis added). This tells us Paul was praying for those who have a living faith in Messiah, evidenced by love.

The older I get in the Lord, the more I see that the ultimate fruit of the Holy Spirit is love, which will remain forever. All the gifts of the Spirit will pass away, 1 Corinthians 13 tells us, except faith, hope, and love, with love being the greatest of these. Jesus said, "By this all men will know that you are My disciples, if you have love for one another" (John 13:35). Knowledge puffs up, but love edifies (1 Cor. 8:1). If we're walking in love and the love in our lives is increasing, then we're truly on the journey of faith in Messiah.

We can't take for granted that we're walking in love. Paul told us, "Test yourselves to see if you are in the faith; examine your-selves!" (2 Cor. 13:5). We can't just go coasting through life without looking at ourselves to see whether we're in the faith. And I think one of the ways we can examine ourselves is by asking ourselves if we are walking in love and if our love is increasing.

Now, none of us is perfect. I often feel like the apostle Paul, who said he was chief among sinners (1 Tim. 1:15). I recognize failings in my life. But what I also see is that I'm walking in greater love and unity today than I was last year, and much more than the year before that. We're on a journey to perfec-tion, and the perfection is love. So if you have a living faith in Yeshua and you're walking in love—not that you're perfect but you're striving to walk in love and you're growing—you can have confidence this prayer is for you.

Wisdom and Revelation in the Knowledge of Him

Paul then cut to the center of his prayer in verse 17, asking "that the God of our Lord Jesus Christ, the Father of glory, may give to you a spirit of wisdom and of revelation in the knowledge of Him." Notice that Paul calls upon "the Father of glory." As I noted in chapter 10, Paul began his many letters to the early churches by saying, "Grace to you and peace from God our Father and the Lord Jesus Christ." (See Romans 1:7, 1 Corinthians 1:3, 2 Corinthians 1:2, Galatians 1:3, Ephesians 1:2, Philippians 1:2, Colossians 1:2, 1 Thessalonians 1:1, 2 Thessalonians 1:2, 1 Timothy 1:2, 2 Timothy, Titus 1:4, and Philemon 3.) This is also how he began his prayer in Ephesians 1, addressing not only Yeshua but Father God, who sent Jesus to the world.

Sometimes Christians are so focused on Jesus they forget that it's because of the Father's love for them that Yeshua was sent in the first place. The most famous verse in the Bible, John 3:16, tells us that God so loved the world that He gave us His only Son. Who is this God that "so loved the world"? It's the Father of the Messiah Jesus, the One referred to in the Old Testament, or the Hebrew Bible, as Yahweh, which comes from the four Hebrew letters *yud, hey, vav,* and *hey*—YHWH, pronounced as a breathy "Yah-weh," according to most Semitic scholars. This is who Paul was praying to—the God of Israel, who is the Father of glory and the Father of the Lord Jesus Christ.

So Paul said, "[I] do not cease giving thanks for you, while making mention of you in my prayers; that the God of our Lord Jesus Christ, the Father of glory—[Yahweh]—may give to you a spirit of wisdom and of revelation in the knowledge of Him" (vv. 16–17). Paul didn't pray for wisdom just for wisdom's sake. Although wisdom is always good in every respect, Paul prayed specifically that we would have wisdom and revelation in the knowledge of who God is.

Now, beloved, please hear me because this is important: Paul is linking wisdom with revelation. Why? Because revelation is the bedrock the church is being built on. In the Book of Matthew, Jesus asked His disciples, "'Who do people say that the Son of Man is?' And they said, 'Some say John the Baptist; and others, Elijah; but still others, Jeremiah, or one of the prophets.'" Yeshua then said, "'But who do you say that I am?' Simon Peter answered, 'You are the Christ, the Son of the living God.'" What was Yeshua's response to Peter? Jesus said this: "Blessed are you, Simon Barjona, because flesh and blood did not *reveal* this to you, but My Father who is in heaven." And then Messiah said, "I also say to you that you are Peter, and upon *this rock* I will build My church; and the gates of Hades will not overpower it" (Matt. 16:13–18, emphasis added).

I believe the *rock* Yeshua was referring to is the *rock of revelation*. The Bible tells us that everybody who hears and learns from the Father comes to Jesus (John 6:45). So our faith is built on the revelation the Father gives us in the knowledge of Him. It's built on the wisdom to first understand that Jesus is the only way and then to perceive by revelation the mysteries of the Spirit and the kingdom of heaven. The world's mindset tells us that Jesus is one of many paths to God and to be politically and culturally correct. That's not the wisdom or revelation of God.

Our Creator wants us to know Him and understand that He is faithful, trustworthy, and powerful, and as King David said, He desires us to behold His beauty (Ps. 27:4). But to experience this reality, we must ask Him to fill us with the wisdom, revelation, and knowledge of Him. And we can't ask for this just once and think we're done. We must continually pray for God to keep revealing Himself to us.

And when you pray, ask "that the eyes of your heart may be enlightened, so that you will know what is the hope of His calling, what are the riches of the glory of His inheritance in the saints" (v. 18). By praying that you will know more and more what is the hope of your calling, who you are to God, and where you're going, you will enter into the depths of eternal life. Abba (the Hebrew word for *daddy* [Rom. 8:15]) wants you to have answers to the most fundamental questions of your existence: Who am I? Where am I going? And what is my purpose? That's what Paul is praying for us.

Many people want to know their purpose in life, but often they are looking in the wrong place. Your purpose is bigger than what you do for a living. It's bigger than the area of ministry you serve in. Your ultimate calling is God Himself. The Scripture says, "In Him we live and move and have our being" (Acts 17:28). God is the One in whom we find our calling. It's not a ministry assignment but a relationship with Him! Only as we get to know God will we come into the sense of having a divine destiny or knowing who we are.

The Riches of His Inheritance

Paul drilled down on this as he continued in the prayer: "I pray that the eyes of your heart may be enlightened, so that you will know what is the hope of His calling, *what are the riches of the glory of His inheritance in the saints*" (v. 18, emphasis added). Simply put, Paul was praying that you and I would know how precious we are to God the Father. Beloved, inside you there is something so beautiful—more beautiful than a diamond or a sunset. Paul spoke of what's inside us as the riches of God's glory. We are the Father's inheritance.

When Jesus gave His life on the cross, He didn't do it just to forgive us; He did it to marry us! We are His inheritance. We are what He gave His life for. We're what He shed His blood for. It's because of us that He took the nails in His hands and feet and the spear in His side. He did it to redeem us. God didn't send Jesus to the cross just to die for you; He sent Messiah to shed His blood to purchase you—and to marry you.

You are important beyond any words that I could use. Paul is praying that you and I would have revelation to understand how special we are to Father. That is why we are referred to in Scripture as the bride of Christ and the gospel story ends with us at the marriage supper of the Lamb (Rev. 19). Your importance, your value, your significance is so much greater than any validation this world or any person could ever convey. Let me say that again. Our value far exceeds any validation this world could ever give. If we're looking to the world to affirm us, if we're looking to some man or woman, our job, possessions, friends, or bank account to give us a sense of significance, we are going to be utterly disappointed. Neither the world nor anybody in it can ever validate us in a way that measures how significant we really are.

As I have ministered over the years, I have met so many single women who are divorced or have never been married and spend so much of their time and have as their primary focus one thing: looking for a husband. They seem to think, "If I could only find the right man and get married, all my problems would be solved." But I tell these beautiful women of God that there is no man on earth who could ever affirm them in the way Jesus does.

Men often get their validation from their status in life and what they do for a living. They think their profession, wealth, looks, stature, or athletic ability will give them a sense of self-worth and significance. But men, we are so much more significant and valuable than the world or any of these things will ever convey. I don't care if you're the president of the United States; even that pales in comparison to knowing who you are to God Himself, your Creator. This is what Paul was praying for—that we would understand the glory that's in us.

There is something in us that is so incredible and wondrous. Consider how ingenious and sophisticated the human body is. When we begin to overheat, our bodies have a built-in intelligence that causes us to perspire to bring our body temperature back down into a normal range. And when we get an infection, the body creates antibodies to combat the infection. The incredible, divine genius in the human body is fascinating to study—I could go on and on about how brilliantly, fearfully, and wonderfully made we are (Ps. 139:14). From our minds, which are vastly superior to any computer system on earth, to our eyes, which have the ability to see, focus, and perceive light, our bodies reflect God's marvelous design. But what is even more incredible than our physical bodies is who we are inside.

If you've ever read accounts of people who were clinically dead, went to heaven, and came back to recount what they experienced there, you know they often describe feeling their inner person leave their bodies. I've read accounts where people say they remember looking down at their bodies as they were moving toward another dimension. Whether you believe these accounts or not, it is clear that you and I are more than our physical bodies. These bodies are just houses we live in. The person inside the body, the hidden person of the heart—the soul—is the real you, and your soul is so incredible words can't explain it. This is what Paul was praying for—that you would understand the glory of God inside the real you. This real you is God's inheritance and the reason Jesus died to purchase you with His own blood.

So let's keep praying, beloved, that Father God will give us a spirit of wisdom and revelation to understand who we really are and the glory of the One who is in us. We are His inheritance. I pray God will cause us to understand how beautiful we are to Him.

Father loves you so much that He sent His Son to purchase you for Himself so that you could be partners with Him in love.

When you sincerely ask God to reveal these truths to your heart, He's going to answer that prayer every single time because you are praying according to His will.

Resurrection Power

Paul continued this theme in verses 19 and 20, where he asked Father to enlighten us that we would know "the surpassing greatness of His power toward us who believe. These are in accordance with the working of the strength of His might which He brought about in Christ, when He raised Him from the dead and seated Him at His right hand in the heavenly places."

Paul was praying here that you and I would comprehend that the same power Father used when He raised Messiah from the dead is at work in our lives. The same power that came into Yeshua's body while He was in the tomb, brought Him back to life, and raised Him from the dead is at work in you and me. The power of the resurrection is being imparted to us, and Paul wants us to understand this.

That is why it's important to grasp that when we feel down, depleted, or discouraged, we're not going to fall (Ps. 37:24). Why? Because the power that raised Jesus from the dead is at work in our lives. As you and I, by faith and the power of resurrection life, keep going forward, as we keep persevering and pursuing God, even when we feel discouraged, bored, or as though nothing is happening, as we keep putting one foot in front of the other, each day thanking God, giving Him glory, trying to do what's right, and disciplining ourselves—our inner man is going to be strengthened and we will keep getting breakthroughs into greater realms in God's Spirit, our destiny, and eternal life by the power that raised Jesus from the dead.

Resurrection power is unlike any other power. This is why the Bible says nothing we go through—not things past, things present, or things to come—can ever separate us from Father's love (Rom. 8:38). The Bible says he that is born of God overcomes the world (1 John 5:4). Beloved, whatever you may be struggling with, whatever you may have gone through that caused hurt or trauma, I want you to know you're going to recover because the Spirit that lives within you is the same Spirit that raised Jesus from the dead (Rom. 8:11). "For," Scripture says, "a righteous man falls seven times, and rises again" (Prov. 24:16).

There is a power in your life that makes you unconquerable. Even as the grave couldn't hold Jesus down, there is nothing that will ever stop you. That doesn't mean you'll never get knocked down or discouraged. It doesn't mean you'll never have a bad day. But at the end of the day it means you are an overcomer because the power that raised Jesus from the dead is focused on and in you.

You're the apple of Father's eye. That makes you a victor and winner. God's elect will not be defeated.

Maybe you grew up in a home where your parents abused you spiritually, mentally, or even physically. Do you know what? You're going to conquer and be made whole. That which victimized you in the past is not going to hold you forever, even as the grave couldn't hold Jesus. And the reason it's not going to hold you forever is that the power that raised Jesus from the dead, the power that conquered everything, is at work in your life. I speak and release supernatural victory and recovery over you in the name of Messiah Jesus of Nazareth right now.

You're going to get through it. You're going to get over it. And you're going to get beyond it, no matter what happened. Maybe you got fired from your job or you're struggling with low self-esteem. Maybe your spouse cheated or left you and you're so wounded inside you don't know if you're ever going to recover. I want you to hear me: you're going to recover. Again, I speak supernatural recovery over your life right now in the name of Yeshua of Nazareth, who rose from the dead. The same power that raised Jesus from the dead, made Him whole, and then exalted Him to the right hand of God is at work in all God's children's lives—including yours.

We are more than conquerors. If you're sick, call out to God and believe Him for the same power that raised Jesus from the dead to affect your body and restore you to health. God's Word says, "If the Spirit of Him who raised Jesus from the dead dwells in you, He who raised Christ Jesus from the dead will also give life to your mortal bodies" (Rom. 8:11). We walk in resurrection power.

Now, it's important to realize that sometimes Father will bring us through seasons and circumstances in life that can cause us to become weak. Paul learned of this and explained it to us in 2 Corinthians when he said there was a "thorn in his flesh that was causing him distress." We don't know what that thorn in the flesh was for sure. What we do know is that it caused him pain and suffering. He kept praying to Father to take away the thorn that was weakening him. Eventually the Lord spoke to him and said, "No, Paul, I'm not going to remove this problem because in your weakness My power is being perfected." (See 2 Corinthians 12:7–10.) In other words, as God made Paul weak, Paul was left with no choice but to reach out to God for strength. And as Paul reached out to God for strength because he had no power left of his own, the resurrection life of

Messiah Jesus was imparted to him, and through that Paul was made supernaturally strong.

I want you to be aware that sometimes the Lord brings us through trials, wilderness seasons, times of weakness, and even times of pain so that in those times we will call out to Him in a deeper way. In calling out to Him, we receive the resurrection power of Messiah, and that makes us strong, not in ourselves but in His eternal Spirit. Sometimes we take a step backward to go five steps forward. We trade in the power of the flesh for the power of the resurrection life that is in God's Spirit.

This power that raised Jesus from the dead is a present reality. It is more powerful than anything you'll ever face—any circumstance, any relationship, any illness, anything. In Yeshua you are raised and seated at the Father's side. Paul said, "I pray that the eyes of your heart may be enlightened, so that you will know what is the surpassing greatness of His power toward us who believe. These are in accordance with the working of the strength of His might which He brought about in Christ, when He raised Him from the dead and seated Him at His right hand in the heavenly places, far above all rule and authority and power and dominion, and every name that is named, not only in this age but also in the one to come. And He put all things in subjection under His feet, and gave Him as head over all things to the church, which is His body, the fullness of Him who fills all in all" (Eph. 1:18–23).

Father has given us the One who has conquered everything—death, disease, sickness, and all the power of the enemy. He has given us the One that nothing could hold—not the Pharisees and Sadducees, not demons, not death or the grave, not even Satan himself. Yeshua HaMashiach descended to Sheol, then rose to the highest part of heaven to the Father's own right side so that everything now is under His feet. And God gave this One to whom everything is subjected to you and to me, the church. Now, come on! That's something to get excited about!

If that doesn't make us winners, I don't know what does. If that doesn't make us somebodies, I don't know what does. If that doesn't give us confidence, nothing will.

When you know this, you can walk with your head held high. You can stand up straight. You can look people in the eye with confidence and courage because Messiah Jesus, the conqueror, the exalted One, lives in you and me. We are an undefeated people, and even though we may stumble, we'll never fall because Yeshua HaMashiach lives in us, and we are destined to reign with Him for all eternity.

Let's pray what Paul prayed for us—that Father would give us a spirit of wisdom and revelation to understand these eternal realities. Don't just pray it once. Keep praying it. Not all prayers can be answered in an instant. Some prayers are answered over time. After all, the life of faith is not a sprint; it's a marathon. If we pray according to His will, we can be confident we will receive what we ask for.

Chapter 13

STRENGTHENED FROM THE INSIDE OUT

*For this reason I bow my knees before the Father,
from whom every family in heaven and on earth
derives its name, that He would grant you, according
to the riches of His glory, to be strengthened with
power through His Spirit in the inner man, so that
Christ may dwell in your hearts through faith.*
—EPHESIANS 3:14–17, EMPHASIS ADDED

B ELOVED, I WANT you to know that there is more to you
than meets the eye. You have an inner man that the
Spirit of God wants to fill with His power. In Ephesians
3 Paul returns to making intercession for us, this time asking
Father to strengthen us with power through His Spirit in our
inner man (v. 16). As we saw in the previous chapter, there is
a power at work in our lives—it is the same power that raised
Yeshua from the dead. Now, in Ephesians 3, Paul is praying that
we would be strengthened by that power in our inner man.

Over thirty years ago I had a dramatic encounter that made this truth a reality to me. During a time when I was going through a deep season of repentance in my life, the Spirit of God supernaturally filled me from above. He literally came down through my head and took hold of my inner man. I was keenly aware of what was happening; I literally felt the Spirit of Elohim Himself, the Spirit of the living God, travel through my head and take hold of something deep inside me. In the midst of this experience, I knew I had what the Word of God calls our inner man because I felt the Spirit of the Lord come in and actually speak to me through that inner man. That is what Father wants to do for you. He wants to release life and power by His Spirit into your inner man to build you up for His glory.

Paul's prayer in Ephesians 3 reveals eternal truths that reflect God's heart for His children throughout all ages, not just for those who lived when Paul was alive on earth two thousand years ago. As we understand the divine realities contained in this prayer, we will learn how to focus our prayers on the things that matter to God, and we know "if we ask anything according to His will, He hears us. And if we know that He hears us in whatever we ask, we know that we have the requests which we have asked from Him" (1 John 5:14–15).

Experiencing the God of the Now

Paul began his prayer by saying, "For this reason I bow my knees before the Father...that He would grant you, *according to the riches of His glory*, to be strengthened with power through His Spirit in the inner man" (vv. 14–16, emphasis added). Notice that Paul prayed that we would be strengthened in our inner man "according to the riches of His glory." The word *glory* in

Scripture most often refers to God making His power manifest on the earth in a way that human beings actually experience. In other words, more often than not, when we see the term *glory* used in Scripture, it has to do with God making Himself visibly seen or tangibly experienced in human beings' lives.

"It came about as Aaron spoke to the whole congregation of the sons of Israel, that they looked toward the wilderness, and behold, the *glory* of the LORD *appeared* in the cloud" (Exod. 16:10). "The *glory* of the LORD rested on Mount Sinai, and the *cloud* covered it for six days; and on the seventh day He called to Moses from the midst of the cloud. And to the *eyes* of the sons of Israel the *appearance* of the *glory* of the LORD was like a consuming fire on the mountain top" (Exod. 24:16–17, emphasis added).

So what Paul was asking for here is that we would experience the manifest power of God in our inner man. I want you to understand that this is not just a doctrine. It's not just something we hope for. It's not just something we wish for. It is a present reality—we can be brought into the very experience of knowing God's power inside us.

Our Creator, the God of the now, is not just to be studied for what He did in the past. We don't just relate to our God through what He did for Abraham, Isaac, Jacob, Elijah, Peter, James, and Paul. And we don't look to our God just for what He's going to do when He returns or when we're in heaven with Him. Our God is the God of the now, and because of His glory working in the lives of His people, we can experience Him now. He's not the God of yesteryear, and He's not just the God of tomorrow. He's the God of the present. He is the great I Am. So when Paul prays that He would strengthen us through the riches of His glory in our inner man, Paul is asking that our lives would be changed today.

You may have noticed that the people who are most alive for Christ and excited about Jesus are those who have been marked by the God who is *now* with a present-day experience. Somehow the God of glory has made Himself known to them. They may not have had an experience like the apostle Paul had on his way to Damascus when he saw a light from heaven flash all around him and then heard Yeshua audibly speak to him (Acts 9:1–9). And you may have never seen a vision such as I did in 1978, which resulted in my coming to faith. But Abba (Father), Jesus, and the Holy Spirit want to teach you how to intuit God's Spirit on your inside. Father wants us to get in touch with the reality that we have fellowship with Him and that His Spirit is bearing witness with our spirits that He is with us.

The bottom line is that the God who is transcendent and beyond also wants to make Himself imminent or present to us. We can have a grip of Him, knowing that He is the God who is here, that He is the God who is now, that He is the God who is with us, and that He is the God who is in us. Knowing this, we will move forward in power.

This is what Paul was asking of the Father and this is what we can pray for—that as we journey with Him in our present experience, we would be brought into a deeper and fuller relationship with Him that is not just cognitive but is real, alive, vibrant at times, deeply rooted, and internalized.

Finding Peace Within

Once again, Paul said in verse 16 that we would "be strengthened with power *through His Spirit* in the inner man." The Hebrew word translated "Spirit" is Ruach, which means breath. At the end of the Gospel of John, after Yeshua had been raised from the dead, He appeared to His disciples and said, "Peace be with you; as the Father has sent Me, I also send you." Then Messiah *breathed* on them and said, "Receive the Ruach HaKodesh, the Spirit of God." (See John 20:19–22.)

Still today Yeshua is literally breathing His life into His bride through His Spirit. This is why the Bible says we are *partakers of His divine nature* (2 Pet. 1:4). His divine nature has been and is being imparted into our lives.

When Jesus breathed on His disciples and said, "Peace be with you," He was speaking into their inner man, rooting and grounding them in *shalom*, a Hebrew word meaning peace, completeness, and wholeness. Beloved, Father God still wants to fill us with His *shalom*, His peace.

The world is coming at us so intensely and from so many different directions. There are so many things pulling at us that many of us have been drawn out of ourselves. We're looking to the world for affirmation. We're measuring ourselves by the world so we're not really comfortable in our own skin. We're living from the outside in rather than from the inside out, so we're not at peace with who God made us to be.

Currently, the world lies in darkness and is controlled by Satan (2 Cor. 4:4; 1 John 5:4; Rev. 2:13). Ultimately the kingdom of the world will become the kingdom of God (Matt. 6:10; Rev. 11:15). If we are looking to the world to find identity, purpose, meaning, or security, we will never have *shalom*, because God's *shalom* is not of this world. Scripture says, "Peace I leave with you; My peace I give to you; not as the world gives do I give to you" (John 14:27). And "for all that is in the world, the lust of the flesh and the lust of the eyes and the boastful pride of life, is not from the Father, but is from the world" (1 John 2:16).

Too often we think if we just get that job we'll be satisfied, or if we marry a certain person or make a certain amount of money, we'll have more peace. We're looking to the world to give us identity and peace. But the world cannot give us true *shalom*; only Yeshua can. This is why Paul prayed that you and I would be strengthened on the inside, abide in Him, and be comfortable in our own skin.

The place to seek Him is not predominantly on the outside, though we should always pay attention to what God is doing in the outer world. The primary place we experience God is on the inside. As you get strengthened in your inner man by God's Spirit, as Paul prayed, you're going to come into yourself more and more. You're going to sink down more and more into your soul and into abiding deep down in your being where Jesus is. Paul called this place "Christ in you, the hope of glory" (Col. 1:27). In this place, you're going to find a peace that you'll never find in this world, because it's a peace the world cannot give (John 14:27).

Years ago I was with a friend who wanted to go to the park. The person was anxious to get to this place, but after we had been there ten or fifteen minutes, he was anxious to go to the next place. When we got to the next place, in ten or fifteen minutes, he was anxious again to get to the next place. The delusion this person was operating under was that when he got there, he'd have peace. This happens all too often to many of us. We are continually running, thinking that if we can get this or that, or reach a certain place, we'll have peace. But there's a problem with that thinking, because *wherever we go, there we are.* We carry the anxiety with us. We can't escape it by going someplace, eating something, or having a cup of coffee. Paul was praying that we will be strengthened in our inner man by God's Spirit and find the true peace that is within us—Christ in us, the hope of glory (Col. 1:27).

Supernatural Faith That Produces Love

That is why Paul goes on to pray "that Christ may dwell in your hearts through faith" (v. 17). Consider that being strengthened in the inner man causes us to have a supernatural faith. This supernatural faith will cause us to be "rooted and grounded in love." Let's take a step back and put this all in context. Paul prays that Father God would grant you, "according to the riches of His glory, to be strengthened with power through His Spirit in the inner man, so that Christ may dwell in your hearts through faith; and that you, being rooted and grounded in love, may be able to comprehend with all the saints what is the breadth and length and height and depth, and to know the love of Christ which surpasses knowledge, that you may be filled up to all the fullness of God" (vv. 16–19).

It's interesting to note here that being strengthened by God's Spirit in the inner man results first in faith. Faith is a thing. It has substance. It has a spiritual fiber, if you will. It is power. It is the substance of things hoped for, the assurance of things not obtained (Heb. 11:1). It is the confident expectation that what you are hoping for will materialize and fully manifest. It allows us to think God's thoughts, believe what God believes, and desire what He desires. Faith comes from God's Word and from being strengthened on the inside.

When someone is strong inside by the power of God's Spirit,

that person automatically has faith. There's a life within those individuals that gives them faith, and this faith connects them to love because faith believes all things. It's impossible to have faith and fear in the same spot because faith connects us to love, and love casts out fear (1 John 4:18). Fear is the opposite of faith, and faith is the opposite of fear. So when we have faith, it's because of what we choose to believe. Fear believes God may not come through for you. Faith believes God is good and that we are safe and protected in Him.

Children who are raised in safe homes feel safe. They trust in their parents' love. They have faith that tomorrow is going to be a good day. And because they feel safe, because they are experiencing the goodness of their parents, because they know they're loved, children growing up in this type of environment generally are loving kids. Similarly, when we believe by faith in God's goodness, when we believe in His promises, when we believe in His Word, when we know we're safe, protected, and loved, the fruit of love is going to come forth from our lives. The opposite is true also. People who don't trust anyone around them feel unsafe. They're not walking in love. They're walking in self-protection, defensiveness, aggression, ambition, and fear.

Consider John 13:3–5: "Jesus, knowing that the Father had given all things into His hands, and that He had come forth from God and was going back to God, got up from supper, and laid aside His garments; and taking a towel, He girded Himself. Then He poured water into the basin, and began to wash the disciples' feet and to wipe them with the towel with which He was girded."

Stop for a second and think about this. Messiah knew He had come from God and was going back to God and that the

Father had already given Him everything. He knew He was loved. He knew He was secure. He knew where He was going. He knew He had everything. As a result, He was perfectly free to love and serve.

When you and I are strengthened in our faith—when we believe God is good, that God is going to supply all our needs, and that we're going to spend eternity with God—this gives us the ability to open up in love and care about other people. The more I grow in relationship with my Messiah Yeshua, the more I realize that love truly is the central aim. Beloved one, remember that our faith culminates in Revelation 19 with the marriage supper of the Lamb. What is marriage? It's a celebration of love.

Paul prayed in Ephesians 3 that we would "be able to comprehend with all the saints what is the breadth and length and height and depth, and to know the love of Christ which surpasses knowledge, that you may be filled up to all the fullness of God" (vv. 18–19). God's eternal Spirit was praying through Paul that we would know the fullness of His love at work in our lives.

What is more satisfying than that? Truly, love satisfies. We were created for relationship, and when you and I know who we are to the Father, when we know how precious and special we are, when we know that we're chosen and Daddy's going to take care of us, when we know His goodness will surround us all our lives and He will supply all our needs according to His riches in glory—when we really believe these things because we've been strengthened by His Spirit in our inner man—we're going to be free. Amen.

Messiah came to set us free (Gal. 5:1). And Yeshua said in John 8:36, "If the Son makes you free, you will be free indeed." Beloved, as you focus on praying this same prayer Paul prayed in Ephesians 3, you're going to grow in freedom. You're going to grow in love. Your faith is going to be strengthened, and you're going to become a greater and greater blessing to other people. You're going to get breakthrough and be transformed into His likeness from glory to glory.

Many times people focus their prayers on things that are important but temporary. I want to ask you to shift your prayer life and focus on praying for the deeper realities, the things that pertain to eternal life, and the things that matter forever. Father wants you to be strengthened by His Spirit in your inner man, experience His power at work in your life, and be released in His love. When you pray for the eternal truths that God wants to make a reality in your life, you can be sure He is going to answer. You can be confident that He is going to bring about supernatural change in your life, and you will be transformed!

Chapter 14

LOVE THAT ABOUNDS MORE AND MORE

And this I pray, that your love may abound still more
and more in real knowledge and all discernment, so that
you may approve the things that are excellent, in order to
be sincere and blameless until the day of Christ; having
been filled with the fruit of righteousness which comes
through Jesus Christ, to the glory and praise of God.
—PHILIPPIANS 1:9–11

W E'VE DISCUSSED IN previous chapters that the
angels around the throne of God cry out day and
night, "*Kadosh, kadosh, kadosh,*" which is Hebrew
for "Holy, holy, holy." (See Isaiah 6 and Revelation 4.) Each
time the angels are hit with a new wave of God's glory, it takes
their breath away, so to speak, and they have to cry, "Holy," yet
again. They don't cease crying out, "Holy, holy, holy," because
they never stop experiencing more of God. He is inexhaustible,
and each time the angels experience another wave of God's

presence, they respond by crying, "Holy!" That's what our lives are going to be like when we're with Father in heaven. For the rest of eternity we're going to be constantly experiencing the "more of God."

As we look at Paul's prayer in Philippians 1, we are going to explore the "more" Father desires for you and me. I want to encourage you to pray for the things Paul requests in this prayer because they are most important to God. As you echo Paul's petition in your own prayer life, you will become more like Yeshua and you can be sure Father God will hear and answer you because these requests reflect His desires for your life and mine.

The Essence of Everything

Paul's prayer begins, "And this I pray, that your love may abound still more and more" (v. 9). Notice the "more and more" in this prayer. What is Paul requesting that we have "more and more" of? His *love*! I came to faith in 1978, and the longer I walk with Yeshua, the more I realize that love really is the final aim. The Bible says everything is going to fade away except faith, hope, and love, and "the greatest of these is love" (1 Cor. 13:13). There is just no way around it. If we want to become more like Yeshua and walk in His Spirit, we must grow in love.

When we're young in the faith, we're often so zealous about every single doctrine. We fight about eternal security, whether everyone should speak in tongues, whether to be baptized by immersion or sprinkling, and so many other things. Doctrine is important. Truth is important. But sometimes we can be more focused on doctrine than we are on love, and love is the goal. Paul wrote, "If I have the gift of prophecy, and know all mysteries and all knowledge; and if I have all faith, so as to remove mountains, but do not have love, I am nothing" (1Cor. 13:2). We absolutely must have sound doctrine. We must adhere to what the Bible teaches. But the most important area to grow in in God's Spirit and the most important thing to focus on is love. God's Word says, "The goal of our instruction is love from a pure heart and a good conscience and a sincere faith" (1 Tim. 1:5).

Jesus said, "Greater love has no one than this, that one lay down his life for his friends" (John 15:13). This simple but profound verse teaches that love involves sacrifice. To lay down your life for someone else is a sacrifice. Love involves dying to our own will; it involves dying to our flesh and putting someone else's needs above our own. Let's think for a minute about our own lives and consider our closest relationships. Are we dying to self in order to grow in love in those relationships? Are we putting our loved ones' needs above our own? Are we purposing to walk in peace and unity with those whom we are closest in proximity to?

Perhaps you've heard stories about people whose parents were loving to everyone outside the home but showed no love behind closed doors. Maybe that is how you grew up. Perhaps you had parents who were really courteous to the neighbors and those in the community but harsh to their spouse or children. My point is that one way we can gauge how we're growing in love is by asking ourselves how we are relating to the people we're closest to—our spouses, children, parents, and coworkers.

The enemy always wants to bring division, and he often will target the relationships that are the most important to us. He will put accusing thoughts in our minds toward those who are strategically placed in our lives to be a blessing to and to help us grow in grace because the enemy wants to steal, kill, and destroy. He wants to keep us from building the kingdom, and the best way to do that is to keep us from walking in love.

Think about the fact that Paul prayed that our love "may abound still *more and more*" (v. 9, emphasis added). Why the double *more*? It's because as you and I are growing in love, we're actually releasing the love of God through our lives into the earth and being brought into a deeper encounter with Him because "God is love" (1 John 4:8).

It's kind of like this. A body of water that has no outlet will become foul and polluted, but a body of water that has a channel to flow out of is going to stay clean and pure. In a similar way, we can't be who God desires us to be unless we have a river flowing through our lives that is causing us to express the love of God that is being imparted to us. Love by definition must have an object. In other words, if we're not loving people, then we're not walking in God, and we're not abiding in Jesus. The Word of God says:

> Beloved, let us love one another, for love is from God; and everyone who loves is born of God and knows God. The one who does not love does not know God, for God is love. By this the love of God was manifested in us, that God has sent His only begotten Son into the world so that we might live through Him.
>
> —1 JOHN 4:7–9

Now, I know some people find it easier to love than others do. Many men, for instance, find it hard to express love because they think it shows weakness. In some homes it was considered unmanly to show affection, so the men never hugged anyone. They never said I love you. But when we read the New Testament, we see Yeshua's love for His disciples. For example, when He saw all the people grieving around Lazarus' tomb, Messiah cared so much that He wept openly, allowing the people nearby to see how much He loved them (John 11:33–36).

At the last Passover meal Jesus celebrated with His disciples before going to the cross, John, the disciple whom Jesus loved, leaned his head on Yeshua's bosom (John 13:23). Think of how comfortable John must have been with Jesus to have literally leaned his head on Yeshua's chest. Messiah—the Creator of the world, the One who bound Satan and holds the keys to death and Hades, the One who rose from the grave, ascended to heaven, and now sits at the Father's right hand, reigning over everything—is the most masculine being in the universe, and He loves.

It's time for men to break out of the devil's false paradigm that it's unmanly to love. Men, we need to be able to tell people we love them. We need to be able to express affection to people. Being unable to do this actually is a sign of weakness.

We never want to get to a place where we stop growing in love. The love of God is endless. It expands forever. It just gets fuller and fuller, and that's what heaven is going to be like for us. This is why Paul prayed that we would abound in love still more and more.

It's like when you walk into the ocean and the water keeps getting deeper and deeper and is never exhausted. That's what the love of God is like for us. And because we're created in Father's likeness and are members of the body of Yeshua—the church—the Lord wants His love, which is inexhaustible and keeps expanding and growing, to keep expanding and growing in and through our lives.

Real Knowledge and Discernment

What our culture thinks is love is often deceptive. This is why Paul continued by praying that our love would be rooted "in real knowledge and all discernment" (Phil. 1:9). False love is powerful. It feels like love but is rooted in selfish interest, sensuality, or both. If our so-called love is focused on someone because that person makes us feel good or can do something for us, it is not agape, or real, love. Similarly, we read in the Book of James that there are two types of wisdom. There's a wisdom that is pure, godly, full of light, and beautiful. But there's another type of wisdom, or knowledge, that is demonic. (See James 3:13–18.)

In order for our love to grow, we need real knowledge and discernment. Paul wrote, "And this I pray, that your love may abound still more and more in real knowledge and all discernment" (v. 9). Real knowledge is not having insight into somebody's life in order to accuse them. That's not real discernment; that's the spirit of the accuser of the brethren, Satan. God is love, and if the knowledge someone receives causes them to accuse instead of love, it's not from God.

The enemy's false knowledge makes us aware of a person's weakness, vulnerability, and sin, but real knowledge allows us to look past their sin, have compassion on them, and understand why they do some of the things they do. People do sinful things, but we have to be able to look beyond their sin to see their need and love them. For example, many would look at a prostitute and judge her as someone who is living in the lowest state of sin. Obviously prostitution is a grievous sin, but God has real knowledge, so He is able to see beyond the prostitute's sin and recognize her real need.

Instead of simply seeing her sin, Father sees a woman who may not have had a father in her life and whose mother was not really there for her. A lot of the women who get into prostitution had no father to affirm them and tell them they were beautiful. They had no one with them growing up to tell them they had dignity and to help them see themselves through God's eyes. They had no one to help them develop healthy self-esteem and self-respect, so they were vulnerable to the ploys of Satan and lured into a life of prostitution. Because of His love, the Lord sees beyond the sinful act and into the heart of the prostitute. Because He has real knowledge and discernment, He sees why she became a prostitute, and He loves her despite her sin. This is why the Gospel of John includes the story of the woman caught in adultery whom Jesus forgave saying, "Neither do I condemn you; sin no more." (See John 8:1–11.)

Over the years, I have seen how the enemy uses false knowledge and false discernment to bring accusation and create division among believers. We need to guard our hearts against the enemy who is called the accuser of the brethren in Revelation 12:10. When someone hurts us or when we feel threatened by someone or jealousy or envy toward someone, we need to be especially vigilant.

Sometimes people claim their actions are out of love, discernment, or some kind of prophetic knowledge. And because they don't have real knowledge and discernment, they don't recognize that their actions are being fueled by their own hurt; they don't understand that what is happening is that pride rose up, the enemy got in, and now the devil is giving them false, demonic knowledge about someone. They're coming against that person with all types of hateful accusations, and they think their knowledge is coming from God and that they're doing His work by spreading rumors and trying to destroy a brother or sister in the Lord. That is not real discernment. Real knowledge and discernment produce love.

People with real knowledge and discernment practice self-discipline by stopping before responding in pride or anger to someone who hurt them. Real discernment causes them to say, "You know what? I realize what's going on here. I recognize this as you, Satan, and I reject you. I come into agreement with the truth. I come into agreement with real knowledge—the love of God that covers a multitude of sins—and I'm going to strive to forgive. I'm going to strive to overcome evil with good and speak blessing instead of insults. I'm going to strive to walk in love as Yeshua did because I want to be like Him."

This was Paul's prayer for you and me in order "that [we] may approve the things that are excellent" (Phil. 1:10). This gets to the heart of the matter. When we practice walking in love and keeping the enemy out when he tries to get in, we're able to discern good from evil and approve that which is excellent. We're able to follow Jesus' way instead of getting tossed here and there all the time by our emotions and circumstances. The author of the Book of Hebrews wrote that the mature "have their senses trained to discern good and evil" (Heb. 5:14).

Guard Your Thoughts

Our minds are like receivers that can pick up the spiritual atmosphere around us, and the enemy seeks to use this against us. He works by trying to project his own thoughts and his own way of thinking into our minds. Again, our minds are like antennas, and we can either be tuned into the Holy Spirit, or we can be tuned into the forces of darkness. And if we don't guard our hearts and discipline our minds, the enemy is going to find a way to project his thoughts into our minds and hearts. When I was younger in my faith, little things would get me off track. It might just be that I came home really tired or stressed, but that made it easier for the enemy to attack. He would start by putting a thought in my mind about someone close to me, and that thought would put me in a flow that would produce division.

In those early years when I didn't realize what was going on, I would fall into the enemy's traps. But as I got older and became more discerning, I started practicing denying my flesh, and I started treating the significant people in my life with greater love regardless of whether I "felt" good or not. As many of us have heard, love isn't first a feeling; love is a decision. God didn't say, "Whosoever feels..."; He said, "Whosoever will..." As human beings created in God's image, we have the power to choose. We can choose to walk in love. We can choose to put others first and discipline our thoughts, words, and actions so we reflect God's heart toward those closest to us. When I began to choose to walk in love, I was able to recognize when a thought wasn't from Him, pull myself back, and get into agreement with love.

Perhaps you have a problem with someone, and you know you are part of the problem because you have not been in agreement with God's thoughts. Instead, you've been in agreement with thoughts of accusation, which come from Satan, the accuser of the brethren (Rev. 12:10).

Let's repent right now and say, "Father God, forgive me. I repent. I've been selfish. I've had ill-will. I've been in agreement with evil and negativity. I know I'm not walking in love in my relationship with [name the person]. But right now, Father God, by Your grace I'm going to overcome evil with good, and I'm going to practice love. I'm going to seek to restore this relationship by rejecting thoughts of accusation and reaching out in love, in Yeshua's name." This is related to Jesus' command to love our enemies (Matt. 5:43–48).

Maybe it's not just others you've entertained negative thoughts toward. Perhaps you've listened to the enemy's false knowledge about you. Jesus said the second greatest commandment is to love others as we love ourselves (Matt. 22:39). It's hard to love others when we don't love ourselves. If we want to silence the accuser in our own lives, we must come into agreement with the truth and believe that Father loves us.

Satan accuses because he wants to incriminate us; he wants us to believe we're something other than forgiven, loved, and chosen by God. But Messiah's love for us took Him to the cross. He paid the price for our sins and cleansed us by His blood. First John 4:19 says, "We love, because He first loved us." You are loved by the Father, and He wants you to receive His love. Father cherishes you. He loves you unconditionally. He created you in His own image, and His Spirit resides in you. He sees Himself in you, and you are beautiful to Him. When you choose to stand in agreement with this truth, the enemy won't be able to torment you with his accusations, and you will be free to both receive and give love. So I want to encourage you to purpose from this day forward to walk in love—for God, for yourself, and for others.

Beloved, in order to abide in Jesus, we need to abide in love. As you and I recognize that love is the straight-and-narrow way that leads to life and we learn to reject thoughts of accusation against ourselves and other people and choose love instead, we're going to be able to prove what is excellent and walk in the righteousness of Messiah Jesus.

Chapter 15

A PRAYER FOR SPIRITUAL WISDOM AND UNDERSTANDING

For this reason also, since the day we heard of it, we have
not ceased to pray for you and to ask that you may be filled
with the knowledge of His will in all spiritual wisdom and
understanding, so that you will walk in a manner worthy
of the Lord, to please Him in all respects, bearing fruit in
every good work and increasing in the knowledge of God.
—COLOSSIANS 1:9–10

DO YOU BELIEVE God is active in your life? Beloved,
Father is always working behind the scenes of our lives.
He wants us to have faith and believe this. Knowing
that God is always at work will inspire us to press in by His
Spirit to discover Him in a deeper way. Scripture says, "Work
out your salvation with fear and trembling; for it is God who
is at work in you, both to will and to work for His good pleasure" (Phil. 2:12–13). The apostle Paul understood this, and

in Colossians 1 he prayed in partnership with his young protégé, Timothy, that we too would know this reality in a richer dimension.

As we examine Paul's prayer in Colossians 1, I believe you will discover the lordship of Yeshua is much weightier than you realize. When we are filled with the knowledge of Messiah Yeshua's will, as Paul prayed, it will move us out of where we've been and into the deep waters of God's Spirit. So I want to encourage you to meditate on the revelation in this prayer and ask Father to make these truths a reality in your life because they will empower you to enter more fully into the eternal life to which you have been called in Yeshua.

The prayer begins in verse 9 with Paul writing, "For this reason also, since the day we heard of it, we have not ceased to pray for you." What strikes me just in these few words is how committed Paul was to praying for other people. I don't know about you, but when I examine my prayer life in the light of God's Word and the life of Paul, I find that I don't spend as much time praying for other people as Paul did. Please don't misunderstand me. I care about people and pray for them just as most believers do. Yet when I'm alone, I have to ask myself how much of my time is really spent praying for others and for the church to come forth.

I think this is a challenge most believers face. In fact, some people focus almost all their attention on praying for themselves. They want Father to give them a spouse or a job or a new house or even a spiritual breakthrough. But Father wants our prayers to not be centered just on our own needs. He wants us to go to the next level by going beyond our own ego boundaries to also focus on the needs of others. If we want to be known as people who walk in the love of Yeshua, we can't just look out for our own interests. We have to go to a deeper level by praying for the interests of others, especially for the church at large—for Yeshua's bride to arise and enter into the fullness of her destiny.

So as we look at Paul's prayer in Colossians 1, I first want to challenge you to move your boundaries. Expand yourself in the love of God and begin to pray more, not just for your own needs but also for other people. If we're going to walk in the power of the kingdom, if we're going to walk in righteousness, if we're going to walk in the fullness of the Holy Spirit, we have to move beyond our own ego boundaries and become concerned with other people.

Scripture says, "Regard one another as more important than yourselves; do not merely look out for your own personal interests, but also for the interests of others" (Phil. 2:3–4). I know this is not natural for us. In the natural we're all selfish, but we're new creations in Yeshua. Paul's prayer challenges us to come out of the natural, moving into the supernatural to become like Yeshua, who "did not come to be served, but to serve, and to give His life a ransom for many" (Mark 10:45).

The Knowledge of His Will

Consider this again. When Paul prayed for others, he didn't focus on just the temporal, material things. Those are important, but Paul was focused on the bigger picture. He did not cease to pray that we "would be *filled with the knowledge of His will*" (v. 9, emphasis added). Paul's whole prayer was focused on spiritual realities, that we would be strengthened, increase in revelation, and understand God's will. In other words, he was praying that we would obtain breakthrough in our walk and experiential union with God.

Father wants us to break out of the limitations of our natural minds so we will stop seeing Jesus predominantly in the flesh and instead see Him in the Spirit. Although Yeshua is God clothed in humanity, if you and I see Jesus simply as a human being on the cross, we're missing it. Yes, God came to earth, clothed Himself in humanity, and died on the cross. But the Son of God existed before He was clothed in the flesh. We need to know Him predominantly in the Spirit. Yeshua said if we're going to worship the Father we must worship Him in spirit and truth, and too many of us are bound to the earth. We're bound to the flesh. We're bound to what we see with our eyes, and God wants to take us out of this realm into the realm of the supernatural.

The apostle Paul wrote:

> He is the image of the invisible God, the firstborn of all creation. For by Him all things were created, both in the heavens and on earth, visible and invisible, whether thrones or dominions or rulers or authorities—all things have been created through Him and for Him. He is before all things, and in Him all things hold together. He is also head of the body, the church; and He is the beginning, the firstborn from the dead, so that He Himself will come to have first place in everything. For it was the Father's good pleasure for all the fullness to dwell in Him.
>
> —COLOSSIANS 1:15–19

Becoming more aware of Yeshua's living Spirit will help us to be more conscious of His lordship over our lives. He wants to lead us every day in the practical aspect of our lives. God wants us to know when to speak, what to say, and when to stop. He wants us to know when to come and when to go. Father wants us to be able to navigate through life abiding in His Spirit, but how can we do that unless we have an awareness in the present moment of His will? I'm not talking about knowing His will just because we memorized Bible verses in our heads. Paul prayed that God's people would walk in a supernatural consciousness in the present moment of His will and that we would be able to abide in Him. Jesus said, "He who abides in Me, and I in him, he bears much fruit, for apart from Me you can do nothing" (John 15:5). Our goal is to abide in the Holy Spirit and be conscious every second of God's presence. Yet as Paul said, "Not that I have already obtained it or have already become perfect, but I press on so that I may lay hold of that for which also I was laid hold of by Christ Jesus" (Phil. 3:12).

I want to encourage you to get your spiritual antenna up. Father is the God of the now. He's not just the God of yesterday. He's not just the God who worked in the life of Paul and Timothy and Daniel and Moses and the Old Testament prophets. He's your God. Messiah Jesus said He's the God of the living, and we need to walk in the "now-ness" of God. When we become sensitive to the Holy Spirit in the present, then we can walk, as Paul said, "in the knowledge of His will."

This is a supernatural process. Again, the ability to apply the knowledge of God in our present circumstance doesn't come just from book learning. It certainly comes through knowing the written Word of God, but there needs to be a marriage in our lives between knowing the written Word of God and being sensitive to the ever-present Holy Spirit. That's why Jesus told

His disciples, "It is to your advantage that I go away; for if I do not go away, the Helper will not come to you; but if I go, I will send Him to you" (John 16:7).

God's knowledge is being poured out into the earth every second of every day through His Spirit. Even as the sun continues to give forth its rays, whether we can see them or not, so too the knowledge of God and the power of His Spirit are continuing to be poured out to us. "Day to day pours forth speech, and night to night reveals knowledge" (Ps. 19:2). God's power is ever-flowing toward you and me. But we must become sensitive to His Spirit. And the good news is that we can ask Father for this. We can ask Him to open our hearts and expand our consciousness to be able to perceive His will and have understanding and wisdom wherever we are. Believe this, beloved, and seek it in prayer.

The Gift of Wisdom

Where do we get wisdom? We can't get it from the natural world. It is a gift of the Spirit that gives us deep insight into how to walk, manage life, and apply knowledge. Simply put, wisdom comes from God, and it gives us the insight we need to make the right choices.

There are so many different things we could be thinking about, so many things we could be focusing on, and we have an opportunity to choose what we're going to think about. But many times we just let thoughts run through our minds. We don't ask where they came from. And often the filter in our minds that creates those streams of thought is the result of some type of trauma or fearful experience. So we have this constant stream of thoughts that is sometimes fear- and anxiety-driven, and it just pushes us in life. But when we have wisdom, we begin to pay attention to our thoughts. And as we look to the Lord, He gives us the wisdom and power to change the trajectory of our thoughts so we can focus on what is good and move forward in Father's good will.

Judaism teaches that wisdom is the attribute of God through which all His emanations or anointings flow. In the Book of Proverbs, Yeshua is personified as wisdom.

> Wisdom shouts in the street, she lifts her voice in the square...."Turn to my reproof, Behold, I will pour out my spirit on you; I will make my words known to you."
> —PROVERBS 1:20, 23

Everything must be filtered and regulated by wisdom. Feelings are good; the body is good; relationships are good. But in order for us to reach a balance where we're walking in truth, we need to process all of our experiences through wisdom and not be ruled by our feelings.

Feelings, of course, are very important. They make us feel alive. But if our feelings control us rather than wisdom, revelation, and a knowledge of God's will, we're going to fall on our faces. We're going to get shipwrecked. We're going to go astray. We're going to chase after illusions. We're going to chase one feeling after another, and when we get to the end of our lives, we're going to see behind us a trail of destruction. If our feelings are not filtered through a mind that has a knowledge of God's will and a spirit of wisdom and understanding, we are not going to be stable, become spiritually strong, or grow in the stature of Yeshua.

Beloved, if we want to go deeper, we need to become more

aware of what we're thinking about on a daily basis. We have the power to choose our thoughts. This is key to our transformation. We have to become aware of what we're thinking and be willing to let God shift what needs to be changed. In the creation account in the Book of Genesis, God brought light out of the darkness, and the same thing happens in our lives. When we examine ourselves, we may see evil. We may have to admit something needs to change. But if we're willing to humble ourselves and let the Holy Spirit do what He wants to do, from that darkness He'll bring forth light. As we begin to pay attention to our thoughts and motives and continually talk to Father God, He's going to transform us and we're going to know His joy in deep places. The Word of God says, "But all things become visible when they are exposed by the light, for everything that becomes visible is light" (Eph. 5:13).

To Walk Worthy of the Lord

In verse 10 Paul reveals why he prays for us to have wisdom and understanding: "so that you will walk in a manner worthy of the Lord, to please Him in all respects." There's a lot of teaching today on grace, and I believe in grace 10,000 percent. We're saved only by the grace of God; even our faith is a gift of God. But if all we ever hear is that Jesus has done it all through His Son and we never hear that we are in partnership with God and that we need to respond to what Yeshua did, then we've missed the boat. Paul prays that we would "walk in a manner worthy of the Lord" and "please Him in all respects." Obviously, our choices and will have some part to play in this. We are not robots; we are called to "work out our own salvation with fear and trembling" (Phil. 2:12).

Too many of us only hear about God answering our prayers. We're told if we have a need, turn to Jesus. If we're sad, turn to Jesus and He'll make us happy. If we need a job, turn to Jesus and He'll give us a job. If we need a husband or a wife, turn to Jesus; He will give us a spouse. Whatever we need, turn to Jesus, and He'll give us a better life. Praise God, Yeshua does answer our prayers for these types of things and all types of things. But unfortunately, people often aren't hearing the other half of the story, that God doesn't save us just to fulfill us; He saves us for His glory.

Scripture says:

> He chose us in Him before the foundation of the world, that we would be holy and blameless before Him. In love He predestined us to adoption as sons through Jesus Christ to Himself, according to the kind intention of His will, to the praise of the glory of His grace.
>
> —EPHESIANS 1:4–6

Father wants our lives to reflect His glory. It's not first about us, but it's first about Him. "For from Him and through Him and to Him are all things. To Him be the glory forever. Amen" (Rom. 11:36).

Paul's burden is that we would "walk in a manner worthy of the Lord." Stop for a second and ask yourself, "Am I walking in a manner that's worthy of the Lord who called me?" When we wake up in the morning and consider the trajectory of our hearts, let's ask ourselves, "What am I trying to accomplish? What is my goal today? What am I thinking about?" Is your heart saying each morning, "Father God, my goal today is to walk in a manner worthy of You, to please You in all respects"?

I try to hold that mirror up to my face all the time and ask myself if the way I'm handling myself is pleasing to God. Is my life a witness to Yeshua? Walking with Jesus is not about us feeding the flesh. It's not about us just satisfying our own wants and desires. It's about us "walk[ing] in a manner worthy of the Lord."

To "walk in a manner worthy of the Lord" involves holiness. The Hebrew Scriptures speak about the beauty of holiness. Holiness is beautiful. The Bible says we stand holy and blameless before Him in love (Eph. 1:4). The Hebrew word for *holiness* comes from the word *kadosh*, and it means to be separate. So if we're walking as Paul prayed for us to, in a manner that's worthy of the Lord, that means we're living a holy lifestyle, and by definition to walk in holiness means to be walking in a way that's separate from the world.

When we are walking in holiness, the name of Yeshua will always be on our lips. We will be a sweet and fragrant aroma of Jesus to the world around us. We will talk about Messiah Yeshua openly and publicly, we will love Him openly and publicly, and we will praise Him openly and publicly. Sure, some will scorn us, but Jesus said, "Blessed are you when people insult you and persecute you, and falsely say all kinds of evil against you because of Me. Rejoice and be glad, for your reward in heaven is great; for in the same way they persecuted the prophets who were before you" (Matt. 5:11–12). "Indeed, all who desire to live godly in Christ Jesus will be persecuted" (2 Tim. 3:12).

To Be His Witnesses

There's a price to pay for walking in a manner worthy of the Lord. There's a price to pay for following Jesus. Yeshua said, "If anyone wishes to come after Me, he must deny himself, and take up his cross and follow Me" (Matt. 16:24). Paul wants us to be empowered to walk in spiritual revelation and divine insight so we'll walk in a manner that's worthy of the Lord. And part of this is carried out when we're living in this world as His witnesses.

Paul said in 2 Corinthians 5:20 that we are ambassadors of God in the world, encouraging, begging, and entreating people to be reconciled to Him through Yeshua. He wrote, "Therefore, we are ambassadors for Christ, as though God were making an appeal through us; we beg you on behalf of Christ, be reconciled to God" (2 Cor. 5:20). We can't shrink back from being a witness because Jesus said, "Whoever denies Me before men, I will also deny him before My Father who is in heaven" (Matt. 10:33).

Many of us want an experience with the Ruach HaKodesh, the Spirit of God. But if we're going to enter into an experience of fullness with God's Spirit, we have to be willing to pay the price for which He rests in us. Part of this price involves being willing to put Jesus first, which includes not denying Him in front of the world. If you're going to please God, beloved, you need to be bold and be a witness for Him. Carrying the message of Yeshua into the world is a privilege. This is one of the greater works Yeshua said you and I would do (John 14:12). Jesus said, "As the Father sent Me, so also now I send you. Go therefore, telling people to be baptized in the name of the Father, the Son, and the Holy Spirit, making disciples wherever you go." (See John 20:21 and Matthew 28:19.) Everybody can share the gospel with someone, and we must do so, because this is part of walking in a manner that is worthy of the Lord and pleasing to Him.

To Bear Good Fruit

Paul also prayed in this prayer that we would "[bear] fruit in every good work" (v. 10). In Matthew 25, Jesus shared a parable about a landowner who gave talents to people in his kingdom. Yeshua said one man received ten talents, another was given five talents, and another received just one talent. In each of the examples Yeshua gave in the parable of the talents, He was expecting the person who had been given talents to do something with them—to do good works—so those talents would multiply.

Ephesians 2:10 tells us that "we are His workmanship, created in Christ Jesus for good works, which God prepared beforehand so that we would walk in them." In other words, every day we're to be looking for and creating opportunities to do good works by loving and witnessing in Yeshua's name.

He's going before us, creating opportunities for us to do good works. And because we've been born of the Spirit of God and we've been given the ability to create something out of nothing, we also can create good works. For example, you may be in a conversation with a group of people and everything they're talking about is worldly and secular. You can interject and speak life into that conversation. If they're gossiping about somebody, you could change that by saying something good about the person. You can turn the conversation from the realm of darkness and negativity into the realm of light, and dispel the darkness. You can shift the atmosphere from one that is earthbound and demonic into an atmosphere that is heavenly, godly, and life-giving by your words. You can create. You can initiate. God's

Spirit is in you, and you have been given the ability to do this thereby creating a good work, which you will be rewarded for.

We're born of God's Spirit, and that is a creative Spirit. Jesus told the man with the withered hand to stretch forth his hand, and as he did, that hand was restored (Mark 3:1–6). The same Spirit that re-created that man's hand dwells in us. As we're open to the Spirit of eternal life that resides within us, He's going to come forth through us to create life wherever we go, even where there's darkness.

I want you to hear me. You are supernatural. You carry creative life. The eternal Spirit of God Himself lives in you, and as you walk in boldness and obedience, as you walk in a manner that's worthy of your calling and make your heart's ambition to please the Lord, you're going to create light in the darkness wherever you go. People are going to see Jesus in you. People are going to put their faith in Him because of you. You're a conqueror. The boldness of Father is on you. Jesus lives in you, and you carry the light.

I want to challenge you in the love of God to live in such a way that you're manifesting the kingdom wherever you go. With the wisdom, knowledge, and revelation of Yeshua within you, you have the power to transform the spiritual climate wherever you go. Life primarily is happening in the spiritual realm. We're so caught up in the natural world with what we see, touch, taste, and smell that we think that's what life is predominantly about. But the truth is that life is more of a spiritual reality. The invisible is greater than the visible. This is why Hebrews 11:3 says, "What is seen was not made out of things which are visible." Everything we do, say, and even think influences the spiritual atmosphere around us. I've had people walk in my home and say, "Wow, it feels happy in here." It's not that I'm always "ha ha" happy. I'm not. But they felt a general sense of happiness in my home because of all that had been thought there, all that had been said there, and all the deeds that had been done there. My point is simply that we have power to create, influence, walk in good works, bear fruit, and please God!

Again, bearing good fruit is not simply a matter of doing works. Bearing good fruit has to do with what you are releasing by your spirit. You are first a spirit, and you have been born again by the Spirit of God. Your body is just the encasement that hosts your spirit right now. You have to understand that you are a supernatural son or daughter of God, and because you have the Spirit of God, you have the ability to bear fruit in the spirit world. You can release peace by your spirit. You can release a blessing by your words. When you speak words by the Spirit, you can build up, but if you release words that come from a defiled spirit, the spirit of the age, you will tear down.

God has given you His Spirit to bear good works, and if you carry yourself in the Spirit of God, even your presence carries with it the capacity to produce trust, love, peace, safety, and a consciousness of God's presence. Wherever you go, you can leave an imprint in that atmosphere, and the people you have been with can be changed for the better.

This is just one example of what it means to bear good fruit. Approximately twenty-five years ago, I was working for a financial services company that sold insurance and investments. The Columbus, Ohio, office out of which I worked employed approximately twenty agents, and at the time I was the low man on the totem pole because I had not been there long. One day, six or seven of the agents were talking in the hallway, and

I walked over to join them. I don't remember what they were talking about, but what I do remember is that I began to witness for Jesus, and it seemed to me at that time that I was completely ignored.

Years later, after I had left the financial services industry and was in full-time ministry, I was a guest speaker at an old country church in rural Ohio. When I arrived at the church, I met the pastor and he showed me where to put up my display. It was just the two of us there at the time, and the pastor came to me and said he had to leave for about a half hour because someone called and wanted to attend the service but had no ride. So the pastor left to go pick this person up. About a half hour later, the church door opened and in walked the pastor with the visitor.

I couldn't believe who walked in with the pastor. It was one of the top producers at the financial services company I had worked for. This man was in the group that day years earlier when I had been witnessing for Jesus. But his life had taken a dramatic turn. He had started dating a prostitute and ended up getting seduced into her cocaine habit. He became so addicted that he ran out of money and forged a check to get more drugs. He was arrested for forgery, and while he was in jail he remembered my witness. The Holy Spirit had used my witness years later while the man was incarcerated to bring him to faith. We just never know how God may use us.

You can influence the world around you with your spirit, creating love, joy, and peace and bringing the spirit of counsel wherever you go.

Increasing in the Knowledge of God

Have you ever gotten burned out with where you are in God? Do the things that used to excite you no longer excite you? Are you feeling that where you are is stale and you need something new from God? I've been there. I sometimes get a revelation from God, and I work with that revelation. I'm excited about that revelation, I put that revelation into practice, and it fuels me for a number of months, a number of years even. But eventually I can no longer live on yesterday's manna. Like the children of Israel in the wilderness, I need fresh manna for today.

Paul prayed that we would be "increasing in the knowledge of God" (v. 10). God intends to bring increase in your life. His purpose is not just to leave you with yesterday's manna but to give you something fresh. If you're feeling stale with where you are in the Lord right now, if everything just kind of seems like "been there done that," if everything seems boring for you, I have good news. Father God is going to give you something new and restore the joy of your salvation.

As you continue to surrender yourself to God, He is going to bring you into a new dimension of experiencing His eternal life. But you must be willing to let go of where you are. If you're so concerned with what people think about you that you won't step out of the crowd to follow God wherever He leads, as Abraham did, if you don't have the conviction and courage to do that, you're going to stay stuck, stagnant, and bored, and you won't experience the fresh thing. But if you're willing to follow the Holy Spirit's leading in your life—which is sometimes subtle so you have to pay attention—if you're willing to let go and follow Him even though it may lead you out of your comfort zone,

He's going to bring you into something fresh, new, and better. You're going to experience "increase."

We all come to places in our lives where we get bored. Things get dry and become has-beens. That's OK. When those seasons come, that means you need something new. But if you're going to enter into the new thing, you have to come out of the old thing. Israel couldn't have entered the Promised Land if they hadn't let go of the old thing. They had to let go of the old thing before they could enter into the new. The word Hebrew carries the idea of one who has crossed over or passed through. The Hebrews had to cross the Jordan to enter into the Promised Land. We are continually being called into a new and deeper place in God's Spirit.

You and I must have an experience like Abraham did. Abraham was willing to leave what made him comfortable and secure in the natural because he trusted God to lead him into something better. So many believers aren't experiencing something better because they don't trust God enough to let go of where they are. They won't let go of their comforts, and they're too afraid of being different and standing out. They're afraid of what people will think of them. God can't do anything for them because they're holding on to where they are.

If you're holding too tightly to where you are, how can you come out of that place and into a new thing? If a child is grasping an old, beat-up toy and won't let go, how can they receive the brand-new toy their parents want to give them? The child wants the brand-new toy and eventually must realize they have to let go of the old in order to receive it. You too have to trust Father God, let go, and follow Him where He leads you. Even though that's scary, there's a reward on the other side.

Beloved, this is the way of eternal life. It's an adventure in God.

It's a journey in the spirit, and each of us must make our own journey. In some respects, we have to go alone. But if we're willing to trust that God is leading us, even when we're afraid, and let go to follow Him, we're going to get where God wants us to go!

Steadfast in the Lord

Paul continued by praying that we would be "strengthened with all power...*for the attaining of all steadfastness and patience; joyously*" (v. 11, emphasis added). God wants to ground you and me. We are in the process of being made steadfast in Jesus Christ. Yes, feelings come and go. Some days we feel up, and some days we feel down, but despite that there needs to be a consistency in the way we walk and a patience in the way we handle life. Father wants us to come to a place where we don't panic when bad things happen, where we don't let go when it feels like we can't hold on. He wants us to have a steadfastness and a patience that make us secure and secures us in the Lord.

We're being held in the grip of God, and He releases strength into our lives to ground us, producing patience and steadfastness. This supernatural strengthening in our souls by the Spirit will create in us a joyfulness. Many years ago while I was sleeping one night, I suddenly became aware of the pain that was in my soul. Even though my eyes were still closed and I was in a semi-dream state, I knew I was having an experience with the Lord. And all of a sudden, whatever veil that prevented me from feeling on an everyday basis the pain that I carried deep within me suddenly was torn open so that I felt an inner pain I didn't even realize was there.

Then an angel spoke to me and said, "You're on the right path." And I replied, "If I'm on the right path, why does it hurt so much?" Then the angel said, "Well, maybe if you cooperate more, it wouldn't hurt so much." The angel's voice was very kind. There was no condemnation in it, but his words struck me. And I said to the angel, "When will I be happy?" Then the Spirit of the Lord spoke to me and said, "When you get strong, then you'll be happy."

Beloved, as God grounds us and we get strong in Him, a joy-fulness is going to break through. I believe there are two elements to joy. One the one hand, there are some things that aren't explainable. For example, you can't explain how God can be self-existent, how He has always been. That's unexplainable; it just is. There is an aspect of joy that is unexplainable in the sense that it is simply the result of a supernatural strengthening and a rising from within that is generated solely by the supernatural impartation of God into our souls. That is one element of joy.

The other element of joy is hopefulness that can be tied to our cognition. It involves thinking and believing the right things. For instance, I'm struggling right now because I see so many doors around me shutting as the world is becoming less and less open to the good news of Messiah and more hostile toward God's Word and His ways. I'm having to transition my thinking from trying to take joy or excitement from something I'm seeing happen in the natural world to totally focusing on what the Bible says should give me hope, which produces joy. So I'm going back to the Scriptures, which talk about "looking for the blessed hope and the appearing of the glory of our great God and Savior, Christ Jesus" (Titus 2:13), and reminding myself that the blessed hope is Jesus' return.

Knowing deep down in our souls that whatever is happening in our lives is all working together for good produces in us a supernatural rest and joy in God. This supernatural strengthening in our souls by the Spirit will create in us a joyfulness. Again, there is a joy that is a supernatural impartation of uncreated life into our being that rises up from within, a strength that has no explanation other than God. And there's a joy that comes through the renewing of our mind, which allows us to align our thoughts with God's light and truth and know that whatever is going on is working for our good. These two together produce joy and breakthrough.

In All Things Give Thanks

The result of all that God has done is that we'll walk around thanking and praising the Lord—"giving thanks to the Father, who has qualified us to share in the inheritance of the saints in Light" (v. 12).

This is so important. We see in Scripture that God often gets upset with people when He blesses them and they don't respond by being thankful. In the Torah, we see that the Lord was upset with Israel because they did not rejoice for all the good things He had done for them.

> Because you did not serve the LORD your God with joy and a glad heart, for the abundance of all things; therefore you shall serve your enemies whom the LORD will send against you, in hunger, in thirst, in nakedness, and in the lack of all things; and He will put an iron yoke on your neck until He has destroyed you.
>
> —DEUTERONOMY 28:47–48

We don't want the Lord to stop doing good things for us because we don't rejoice when He does. So we must be conscious of God's goodness toward us. We need to count our blessings daily and not take them for granted. When you're eating, for example, slow down and recognize that it's a gift from God to you that you're able to take pleasure from what you're eating. Father and Yeshua want us to walk through life thankful and rejoicing, even in the difficult times.

I know we go through battles. I know we go through tough times. But we have a choice. When we're in tough situations, we can still give God thanks by faith. We can still say, "Father, thank You. This might be a challenge, but I choose to love You. I choose to be grateful. I choose to believe that You're doing something good in my life right now."

During a recent trip to Colorado, I was driving down a road that was riddled with deep potholes, had high boulders, and was rather isolated. As I was driving down this road, I was thinking, "Man, this would be a scary place to get a flat tire. What would I do?" Well, wouldn't you know, I got a flat tire. But you know what I did? I said, "Baruch HaShem," which is Hebrew for "Bless the Lord." I said, "Father, I receive this from Your hands. I believe You're causing everything to work for good. Father, I know You're with me. There's a purpose in this, and I'm going to give You glory. I'm going to thank You in this. Your Word says, 'Give thanks to God in all things, for this is His will for you in Christ Jesus,' so I'm going to rejoice right now and believe You're in this and doing something good."

I had the wisdom and understanding to know that God can use all things and cause good to come from them. Even the world was birthed out of darkness (Gen. 1:1–3). There was darkness before there was light. So in everything we go through, we can thank God, knowing He brings light. So I thanked Him as

I was changing the tire, and in that process I brought joy to His heart, because I trusted Him.

This is the way God wants us to live. When we have wisdom and understanding, we can give thanks in all things. We belong to King Yeshua. He is intimately involved in our lives, closer even than our own breath, and He wants us to trust Him and thank Him for all things. Scripture says, "In everything give thanks; for this is God's will for you in Christ Jesus" (1 Thess. 5:18).

The Lord says, "Don't look back. Look forward." Paul said he pressed toward the mark in Christ Jesus, forgetting what lay behind and pressing onward and upward toward the goal (Phil. 3:13–14). There's always more, and it can always get better.

Many people, perhaps even the majority of people, are unable to change, and we know that oftentimes as people age, they become less and less willing to change. They're less and less flexible. But we need to stay flexible and be willing to be changed so we can experience the heights of walking with Yeshua. God has good plans for us, but we have to let go and follow Him. The things of the world eventually get old. But God's Spirit, as I often say, is always fresh, it's always new, and there's an adventure for us in God.

Being "filled with the knowledge of His will in all spiritual wisdom and understanding" is a constant thing. We're not filled just once. It's a continual filling because life is always going forward. It never stays stagnant. My earthly father once said to me, "The only thing that never changes is change itself." God's life is constantly rolling out, moving, and new. This is why we must rise out of where we've been, because the filling Paul was praying for in Colossians 1 goes on forever. We're continually relying on Father to fill us "with the knowledge of His will in all spiritual wisdom and understanding." So beloved, give Him permission to take control. Let Him do whatever He needs to do in your life. Continue to pursue Him and let Him fill you again and again.

PART IV

Yeshua, Our Redeemer: In Spirit and Truth

Chapter 16

A MODEL FOR PRAYER

Pray, then, in this way: "Our Father who is in
heaven, hallowed be Your name. Your kingdom come.
Your will be done, on earth as it is in heaven."
—MATTHEW 6:9–10

THE LORD'S PRAYER is also referred to as "the Disciples'
Prayer" because it is the prayer Yeshua taught His disciples. This is one of the most familiar passages in the entire
Word of God. Even those who don't embrace the Christian faith
are familiar with this prayer.

All the prayers we've looked at in this book give us insight into
what moves God's heart. But what is so special about the Lord's
Prayer is that it is the one Messiah Jesus Himself taught us to pray.
Yeshua gave us this prayer model from the portion of Scripture
that is often referred to as the Sermon on the Mount. He said:

Pray, then, in this way: "Our Father who is in heaven, hallowed be Your name. Your kingdom come. Your will be
done, on earth as it is in heaven. Give us this day our

daily bread. And forgive us our debts, as we also have forgiven our debtors. And do not lead us into temptation, but
deliver us from evil. [For Yours is the kingdom and the
power and the glory forever. Amen.]"

—MATTHEW 6:9–13

Each line of this prayer is rich with meaning. If we truly
pray according to the principles of this prayer, our lives will be
transformed and we will experience God in an ever deeper way.
So let's examine what this prayer reveals about God's heart and
character and how we should relate to Him.

Our Father...

Yeshua tells us to begin our prayers by saying, "Our Father who
is in heaven, hallowed be Your name. Your kingdom come.
Your will be done, on earth as it is in heaven." Just think about
that for a moment. Here is the Word made flesh, the Son of
God, Yeshua HaMashiach, telling us that we should begin our
prayers by exalting the Father—that we should acknowledge
that God's name is holy and set apart, that He is high and lifted
up, that it is not about us first but about Him. Then we are told
to align our will with His will.

That's not what many churches are emphasizing or what
typically happens in the prayer lives of many people who call
themselves believers. In our culture today, the American dream
and self-promotion have replaced dying to ourselves to follow
Yeshua. Many times believers' prayers don't begin with, "My
Father who is in heaven, holy is Your name; Your kingdom
come; Your will be done." Instead, many prayers begin with,
"God, will You give me this?" "God, will You give me that?" But

if we want to pray in a way that touches the center of God's heart, if we want to pray according to His will, our hearts must cry out, "My Father, who is in heaven, holy is Your name; Your kingdom come; Your will be done on earth, beginning in my life, even as it is in heaven."

For many, walking with God is too much about them and not about God. But when we look at Jesus' life and consider how Yeshua taught us to pray, we see that His message and revelation don't make prayer first about us. It is first about the Father. It is not first about our will; it is first about the Father's will.

Jesus said, "If anyone wishes to come after Me, he must deny himself, and take up his cross and follow Me" (Matt. 16:24). What does it mean to pick up your cross? It means to die to yourself. God's Word says we no longer belong to ourselves. We belong now to the One who gave Himself on our behalf. So we exist in this world not to please ourselves first but to please the One who purchased us by His own blood.

Yet if we're honest with ourselves, that's often not what our walk with God looks like. That's not the nature or character of it. We're basically in our own quest to achieve our dreams, and we want to use God to do that. But that type of spiritual life is radically different from the model Messiah gave us. Yeshua's way calls us to lay down our lives to do the Father's will and deny ourselves to please Him. If we want our prayers to move the heart of God, we have to take very seriously what the Word of God teaches.

Jesus said to pray, "Your kingdom come; Your will be done." Where does God's kingdom start? Where is His will first done? It begins with us in our prayer lives. It begins as we pray, "Lord, have Your way with me. I belong to You. What do You want to accomplish in my life today? What do You want me to work on today? What is Your will for my life?" Beloved, when we're truly following Jesus, our lives are about dying to the flesh and living for the One who lived and died on our behalf.

A gospel that is man-centered rather than God-centered is a false gospel. A message that is more focused on meeting our needs than it is with revealing the glory of God is not what the apostolic writings teach. Remember, Scripture says that in the last days difficult times would come and people would be deceived with a false gospel (2 Tim. 3). Jesus said, "For many will come in My name, saying, 'I am the Christ,' and will mislead many" (Matt. 24:5). God's Word tells us that when Satan comes to deceive the elect, he's going to come as an angel of light. He's not going to come looking like the devil. He's going to come clothed in a false spirit of Christianity.

So I want to ask you, Is the gospel you've been following a gospel that involves picking up your cross, denying yourself, and following Jesus? Is it a gospel that involves dying to self to obey the Lord? Or have you been seduced by the gospel that is all about believing God for what you want without requiring repentance? John the Baptist's and Jesus' first words were the same: "Repent, for the kingdom of heaven is at hand" (Matt. 3:2; 4:17).

Beloved, I believe God is awesome and that He blesses His children. We shouldn't limit how good He is or what He'll do for those who trust Him. But if prayer is always all about you and me, we're not hearing the message Jesus brought. He taught us to pray, "Our Father who is in heaven, hallowed be *Your name. Your kingdom come. Your will* be done, on earth as it is in heaven."

Give Us Daily Bread

Yeshua continues, "Pray, then, in this way...'Give us this day our daily bread.'" He is saying, "Depend on God for everything; He is the One who sustains you." Every day we wake up, we must rely on God afresh and anew. I'm not talking about relying on Him just for a place to live, food on the table, and financial provision, although it certainly includes all these. I'm talking about an attitude of utter dependency on God.

Every day we need God to sustain us afresh by His grace. Every day we need His protection anew. Every day we need Him to fill us with a fresh impartation of His presence and power. Every day we need His angels all around us, protecting us. Every day we need God. Just as we're dependent on the air we breathe to be sustained physically, we need the Spirit of God, the Ruach HaKodesh, every minute of every day in order to truly be sustained. If God were to take His hand off you and me for even a second, we would be snuffed out, just like that.

Messiah wants us to understand that we should become completely dependent on the Father and not try to live on yesterday's fumes. Messiah Jesus is telling us we need to go before the Lord daily and say, "Father God, minister to me today. Inspire me today. Give me fresh bread today." When we have that posture, beloved, life becomes an adventure. Every day brings something new. Every day is a day of growth and transformation. Every day is a day of discovering Jesus in a deeper way. Beloved, let's do what Jesus told us to do. Let's begin our day by putting ourselves in a posture of loving Him. Set time aside each morning to be still before Him. Start each day in the quiet, reading His Word and seeking His face.

Forgive Us Our Debts...

Jesus continues by saying in verse 12, "And forgive us our debts, as we also have forgiven our debtors." You may have heard the verse put this way, "And forgive us our trespasses, as we forgive those who trespass against us." Whatever wording we're familiar with, the idea involves being transparent before God and allowing the Holy Spirit to show us the things in our lives that we need to be forgiven and cleansed of.

Whether you and I realize it or not, our biggest need is to be forgiven of our sin. In Matthew 1:20–21, an angel appeared to Joseph instructing him, "Do not be afraid to take Mary as your wife; for the Child who has been conceived in her is of the Holy Spirit. She will bear a Son; and you shall call His name Jesus, for He will save His people from their sin." Paul wrote, "In Him we have redemption through his blood, the forgiveness of our trespasses, according to the riches of His grace" (Eph. 1:7). There are things in all of our lives that we need to be forgiven of. Perhaps it's pride, selfish ambition, or not treating others in the way they should be treated. The Holy Spirit keeps showing me more and more things in my life that need to change. The more we grow in grace and get closer to God, the more the Holy Spirit shows us things in our lives that we need cleansing from.

It's like looking at something under a microscope. When you first look at the slide you can't see much. But as you begin to turn the amplification on the microscope up, it reveals more and more of what's on that slide. As the power increases on the microscope, you see more and more things on the slide that you couldn't see before. That's the way the Holy Spirit is in your life and mine. As we get closer to God, the light of His Spirit shines into us more and more powerfully. And as this happens, we see deeper and deeper levels of sin. We see things in our hearts that we didn't see before.

Early on in our walk with Yeshua, we likely thought we needed to clean up certain things in our lives. We thought about all the superficial things we did. Maybe it was smoking or drinking or dressing a certain way. We cleaned up all the outer things, and we thought we were OK. But as we move deeper in the grace of God, the Holy Spirit shines deeper into our hearts and minds and shows us our selfishness or pride, or that we're not esteeming others better than ourselves, or that we're relying on ourselves instead of on God. As He does this, we need to agree with Him and say, "Lord, forgive me." We must continually allow the Holy Spirit to show us our sin, agree with Him about it, and ask Him to forgive us.

...As We Forgive Our Debtors

Next, beloved, Yeshua takes us a step further and says, "And now I want you to forgive everybody who has sinned against you." Jesus said, "When you pray, pray in this way: 'Father, forgive us our trespasses *as we have forgiven those who have trespassed against us.*'"

There are many believers who love God but who are also holding a spirit of unforgiveness or offense against someone in their hearts. But Messiah Jesus is teaching us that if we hold on to unforgiveness and offense, we can't touch God's heart the way we have the potential of doing. We can't see God move in power over our lives the way He wants to when we're holding on to unforgiveness because unforgiveness hinders Him from working in our lives.

Yeshua said, "I stand at the door and knock" (Rev. 3:20). God wants to come in, but unless we open the door and receive Him, Messiah Jesus can't enter. He chooses to respect our will. You and I want to see God move in our lives in power, yet to the degree that we have bitterness and unforgiveness toward people, to that degree we're hindering Jesus from being able to come in and fully move in and through our lives and bless us.

Perhaps you think you're not carrying a terrible spirit of unforgiveness. Yet if you really search your heart and think about it, there may be people in your life that you have not forgiven and are holding some type of ill will against. You have what I call an IOU spirit. By that I mean someone in your life hurt you in some way, and because they hurt you, you want to see them hurt. You want to take vengeance upon them because of the pain they caused you. In other words, you'll forgive them after they've paid for it. You're holding an IOU over their life.

But Jesus said, "When you pray, pray in this way: 'Father, forgive us our sins even as we have forgiven those that have trespassed against us.'" Yeshua even went on to say, "If you do not forgive others, then your Father will not forgive your transgressions" (Matt. 6:15). So I want to encourage you right now to search your heart. Maybe it's a parent you're holding unforgiveness toward. Maybe it's a friend who hurt you in the past. Maybe it's somebody at work, a neighbor, your current or former spouse, an ex-boyfriend or girlfriend, or even someone from your childhood. Whoever it was, you have ill will toward this person and want to see him or her hurt. We have to deal with that.

I know forgiving others isn't easy, but let me share with you something that helps me. I imagine Messiah Jesus on the cross.

I see Him with His arms open wide, dying on the cross for our sins. I see the people on the ground laughing and jeering at Him, the ones who spit on Him and pulled out His beard. Yet on the cross, Yeshua looks up to the Father and says, "Father, forgive them, for they know not what they do." (See Luke 23:34.)

Jesus saw those who mocked and scorned Him down on the ground below, living in total ignorance of what they were doing, and He responded to the wrong they'd done to Him by saying, "Father, forgive them, for they know not what they do." So what I do with people in my life who have hurt me and whom I have a difficult time forgiving is I focus my eyes on Jesus. And as I'm looking at Jesus—not at the people who hurt me but at Jesus—I see the people who hurt me in my peripheral vision. My eyes are focused on Jesus, and in my peripheral awareness I am conscious of the person I need to forgive, and I model Jesus. I come into alignment with His heart and His words, and I say, "Jesus, I forgive them." Then I release His forgiveness.

What I've found is that if I don't keep my eyes focused on Jesus and instead look at the person, I may fall into offense again because I'm focusing on how the person hurt me. But when I keep my focus on Yeshua, I'm able to release the person with the same forgiveness Jesus released when He died on the cross. This is very important. If we're going to receive the experience of being forgiven to the fullest degree God wants us to, we have to make a conscious decision to forgive those who have sinned against us.

Lead Us Not Into Temptation

In verse 13 Jesus goes on to say, "And do not lead us into temptation, but deliver us from evil." It is awesome to realize that we can ask the Lord to strengthen us by the Ruach HaKodesh, by the Spirit of God, so that we won't be led into temptation. In other words, we can ask God to protect us from being exposed to an evil that would overwhelm us. We can ask God to protect us from having to deal with an evil that we may not be able to successfully resist for whatever reason—perhaps because we're not mature enough, or we haven't had enough biblical training, or we don't have enough revelation, or we don't have enough faith.

There are some things that you can stand against, but there may be other forces of darkness that you're not quite ready to deal with. You can actually ask the Lord to keep you from being exposed to those situations that will overwhelm you. You can pray, "Father God, protect me from being exposed to evils and temptations that I wouldn't be able to successfully handle. Lead me not into temptation, but deliver me from evil."

Beloved, Yeshua is able to keep us from evil. He is able to keep us living in victory over the darkness. We should ask Him for what He told us we should ask for—to be protected from temptations.

After saying, "Do not lead us into temptation," Messiah taught us to pray, "but deliver us from evil." We need awareness that evil is all around us. In Revelation 2:13, Yeshua said, "I know where you dwell, where Satan's throne is." John said, "The whole world lies in the power of the evil one" (1 John 5:19). Evil is real, and it's all around us. All you have to do is listen to people talk. The criticizing, the complaining, the bitterness, the accusation, the ungratefulness—it's all coming from the realm of darkness. We should pray to be delivered and washed from it. We are the bride of Christ.

Yeshua continues, "For Yours is the kingdom and the power and the glory, both now and forever." Jesus is saying, "Father

God, Your saints belong to You. Don't let them be overtaken by the enemy. Don't let them bring a reproach upon You because Yours is the kingdom, and Yours is the power, and Yours is the glory. They don't belong to Satan but to You." The Lord wants to be glorified in our lives. He strengthens you and me to overcome temptation and evil so that His name will be exalted in and through us. In the end, Satan will not have anything to boast about or lord over us because, again, the kingdom, the power, and the glory belong to Father God, both now and forever.

Jesus said, "Anyone who chooses to do the will of God will find out whether my teaching comes from God or whether I speak on my own" (John 7:17, NIV). In other words, if we want to know whether the doctrine Yeshua teaches is true, we should do it. If you'll put these truths into practice in your life, the Holy Spirit is going to keep changing you from glory to glory. When our prayers are aimed at pleasing and glorifying God (magnifying His name), seeking His will and His kingdom, living in dependency, humbly asking for forgiveness and releasing it to others, and asking for protection from temptation and deliverance from evil, our prayers will be answered.

Chapter 17

SEEK GOD ON HIS TERMS

At that time Jesus said, "I praise You, Father, Lord of
heaven and earth, that You have hidden these things from
the wise and intelligent and have revealed them to infants.
Yes, Father, for this way was well-pleasing in Your sight."
—MATTHEW 11:25–26

N MATTHEW 11:25–26, Jesus makes an unusual declaration.
In this prayer, Yeshua actually thanks the Father for giving
revelation to some and hiding it from others. Again, the exact
words recorded in Scripture are: "I praise You, Father, Lord of
heaven and earth, that *You have hidden* these things from the
wise and intelligent and have *revealed* them to infants. Yes,
Father, for this way was well-pleasing in Your sight" (emphasis
added). Why would Jesus offer up a prayer like this? What can
it teach us about who God is and what moves His heart? What
can we learn from this short and simple prayer of Yeshua about
how to pray in such a way that our prayers are answered?

There are several dynamics that I think are often missed

when people read this section of Scripture. First, I want to point out something that some may find difficult to receive because it challenges the way many of us think. But being challenged by Scripture is not a bad thing. The Word of God often will confront our way of thinking.

In these verses, Yeshua said that the Father's glory was actually hidden by His design from the wise and the prudent. In other words, Jesus thanked Father God for withholding the revelation of His glory from the proud. And this actually brought Jesus joy. As Scripture says, "God resists the proud, but gives grace to the humble" (1 Pet. 5:5, MEV).

Think about this. Yeshua said, "I praise You, Father, Lord of heaven and earth, that You have hidden these things." The "things" He was referring to were the mysteries of the kingdom of God, the mystery of who Jesus was, the understanding of His parables, the operations of the unseen spirit world, the laws of increase and abundance, and all the spiritual principles in God's Word. The Lord didn't give insight into who Jesus was—the Messiah and Son of God—to the wise and prudent. Instead, He hid it from them. In other words, when the wise and prudent looked at Yeshua, they didn't see the Son of the Most High God. They didn't see the Father's only begotten Son. They didn't see the Master of the universe through whom all creation was made. When the wise and the prudent looked at Jesus, they saw only a carpenter's son because Messiah Jesus' identity was hidden from them.

Paul speaks about the same concept when he says, "Consider your calling, brethren, that there were not many wise according to the flesh, not many mighty, not many noble; but God has chosen the foolish things of the world to shame the wise, and God has chosen the weak things of the world to shame the things which are strong, and the base things of the world and the despised God has chosen, the things that are not, so that He may nullify the things that are, so that no man may boast before God" (1 Cor. 1:26–29).

Beloved, how many high-ranking professionals do you know of who love God passionately? How many are in your church? I know there are high-level professionals in many different fields who truly love God. But Paul said there aren't many of them in the grand scheme of things and that God has chosen the foolish things of the world to confound the wise, prudent, and successful.

One Size Doesn't Fit All

We like to think God reveals Himself equally to everybody, but that can't be substantiated by Scripture or even by looking at the historical reality. Some nations have received the gospel while other nations have never heard the good news. The gospel has been preached all across America. It is being preached throughout other continents and nations. Yet in certain parts of the world, very few people have ever heard the message of Jesus preached. So how can we say that everybody is given the same amount of revelation? It's simply not true.

In the Gospel of Matthew, Jesus asked His disciples, "'Who do people say that the Son of Man is?' And they said, 'Some say John the Baptist; and others, Elijah; but still others, Jeremiah, or one of the prophets.' He said to them, 'But who do you say that I am?' Simon Peter answered, 'You are the Christ, the Son of the living God.' And Jesus said to him, 'Blessed are you, Simon Barjona, because flesh and blood did not reveal this to you, but My Father who is in heaven'" (Matt. 16:13–17).

Jesus was saying in essence, Simon Barjona, you are blessed

because the reason you know that I'm the Messiah, the reason you're able to perceive who I am, is that the Father has blessed you with this revelation. It wasn't something people could see on their own. It wasn't something people could simply figure out through common sense. They could only perceive who Jesus was through a gift of revelation. This is why so many didn't and still don't believe in Him. Scripture says, "He came to His own, and those who were His own did not receive Him" (John 1:11).

It brought Yeshua great joy that His Father revealed Himself to the childlike and those the world looked down upon while at the same time hiding Himself from the proud, the wise, and the prudent. Please hear this, beloved: We like to make God just like us. We have our standards, what we think is right and fair, but God doesn't operate the way we do.

Remember Jesus' parable about the owner of a vineyard in Matthew 20? The landowner called forth laborers to work in his field, and some laborers showed up early in the morning and worked all the way from morning until the end of the day. Other workers showed up in the middle of the day and then worked until the end of the day. Some workers showed up three hours before the day was over, and other workers showed up and only worked an hour. So some worked a full day, some worked a half day, some worked only about a quarter of the day, and some worked for only an hour that day.

Now, we would think each one would be paid according to how many hours he or she worked. But Jesus said the land-owner called all the workers forward to be paid at the end of the day, and he began by giving those who had worked only an hour a full day's wages. Then when the last ones came to get paid, they received the same amount. So the ones who had worked only an hour received the same amount of pay as those who had worked the full day.

Those who had worked all day were understandably upset and said, "We worked the full day, this guy worked only an hour, and you paid him as much as you're paying us." It didn't seem fair. But what did the landowner say? "Listen, I paid you what I agreed to pay you. What is it to you if I want to be generous and pay the guy who worked only one hour the same amount that I paid you?" (See Matthew 20:1–16.) In other words, the Father's standard of right is different from human beings' standard of right, and the Father's standard of fairness is different from our standard of fairness.

This is what Paul deals with in Romans 9. Paul said, "It does not depend on the man who wills or the man who runs, but on God who has mercy" (v. 16). He goes on in Romans chapters 9 through 11 to say that much of national Israel did not obtain what it sought, but the elect obtained it, and the hearts of the rest were hardened. Even more to the point, Paul said in Romans 9:13, "Jacob I loved, but Esau I hated." I know this may be hard to process, but if it's in the Word of God, then we must wrestle with it and accept the truth, no matter how difficult.

The minute Paul wrote that the Lord said, "Jacob have I loved, but Esau have I hated," he knew it wouldn't seem right to us. He knew it wouldn't seem fair to us that God would not create everybody the same and give everyone an equal chance. This is why in the very next verse, Paul wrote, "What shall we say then? There is no injustice with God, is there? May it never be!" He knew that when people read what he had just written, they would react to it and think it was unjust. So Paul went on to say, "Who are you, O man, who answers back to God? The thing molded will not say to the molder, 'Why did you make me like this,' will it? Or does not the potter have a right over the clay, to make from the same lump one vessel for honorable use and another for common use?" (vv. 20–21).

We see this concept throughout the Old Testament, the Hebrew Bible, that God does not give the same amount of revelation or favor to everybody. Consider Israel. Did God give Israel special favor, or did He treat all the nations the same? If you know the Old Testament, you know that God showed Israel favor beyond that which He showed to other nations. The Lord said to Israel, "For you are a holy people to the LORD your God; the LORD your God has chosen you to be a people for His own possession *out of all the peoples who are on the face of the earth*" (Deut. 7:6, emphasis added).

We need to walk with God on His terms. We need to get into alignment with God's mind and heart and stop stubbornly requiring that God become like a man and do things our way. If it were up to us, we might say everybody is required to get the same amount of revelation; everybody must get the same opportunity to respond. But Jesus said, "Thank You, Father, for hiding these things from the wise and the prudent and revealing it to the babes."

Beloved, let's get into alignment with a sovereign God. Yeshua said in John 6, "No one can come to Me unless the Father who sent Me draws him....Everyone who has heard and learned from the Father, comes to Me" (vv. 44–45). The Father is the One who gives the revelation, and He gives it to whom He chooses.

Chosen by God

Jesus said, "My sheep hear My voice, and I know them, and they follow Me....My Father, who has given them to Me, is greater than all; and no one is able to snatch them out of the Father's hand" (John 10:27, 29). We need to understand that God has an elect people whom He chose to be His even before the foundation of the world.

Paul wrote:

> Blessed be the God and Father of our Lord Jesus Christ, who has blessed us with every spiritual blessing in the heavenly places in Christ, just as He chose us in Him before the foundation of the world, that we would be holy and blameless before Him. In love He predestined us to adoption as sons through Jesus Christ to Himself, according to the kind intention of His will, to the praise of the glory of His grace, which He freely bestowed on us in the Beloved.
>
> —EPHESIANS 1:3–6

If you believe in Him, beloved, it's because you are chosen. Remember, Jesus said, "You did not choose Me but I chose you, and appointed you that you would go and bear fruit" (John 15:16).

Even as God chose Israel out of all the nations of the earth, so too is there a remnant today chosen according to grace. Beloved, again, if you love Messiah Jesus today, it's because He chose you. It's because the Father revealed Himself to you. It's because the Spirit of God drew you to Yeshua. This should humble us to get down on our knees and give thanks.

It's not our job to determine whether someone will believe or not. Our job is simply to spread the Word. It's the Father's job to reveal the truth to people. It's the Father's job to draw people to Himself. We just have to be obedient and preach the gospel to the ends of the earth. The Father then will take our witness and use it as He wills.

~≈≈≈≈◝

Beloved, let's get into agreement with God and His Word. As we go before God in prayer, let's stop insisting that He do things our way. What He asks us to do might not make sense to you and me. It might not seem fair, but if it's what the Word of God clearly teaches, we must do it. Let's get into alignment with God, dear one. This is the key to seeing our prayers answered.

Chapter 18

IN THE FATHER'S HANDS

And He went a little beyond them, and fell on His face
and prayed, saying, "My Father, if it is possible, let this
cup pass from Me; yet not as I will, but as You will."
—MATTHEW 26:39

O NE OF THE greatest struggles we face as believers in Messiah is the battle to put our lives completely in the Lord's hands by surrendering to His will. Even Yeshua had to consciously choose to do this, as His prayer life shows.

In Matthew 26, Jesus was about to go to the cross. He was in agony, and His soul was troubled. The Bible says that the night before the crucifixion, Jesus was in so much turmoil as He prayed in the Garden of Gethsemane that He was sweating drops of blood. He sensed He was going to have nails driven through His hands and feet, a crown of thorns placed on His head, and a sword pierce His side.

But the greatest pain Jesus was going to endure wasn't physical. It was knowing that He, the undefiled, pure, spotless Lamb of God, was about to take on the wretched, vile sins of the entire world. And not only that, but He was also about to take into Himself all of our sicknesses and diseases. As Isaiah prophesied, "He was pierced through for our transgressions, He was crushed for our iniquities; the chastening for our well-being fell upon Him, and by His scourging we are healed" (Isa. 53:5; see also Matthew 8:16–17).

We can't imagine how miserable that must have been for Yeshua, how defiled He had to become for our salvation. Scripture says, "He made Him who knew no sin to be sin on our behalf, so that we might become the righteousness of God in Him" (2 Cor. 5:21). That's what was about to happen to the sinless Lamb of God. Yeshua was about to take on the sin of the whole world and bear God's righteous judgment of our iniquity so we wouldn't have to. That's why He sweat drops of blood as He agonized in the garden that night. He was about to face something more painful than you or I can ever imagine.

As Yeshua was facing this huge mountain, He fell on His face in the Garden of Gethsemane and prayed, "Father, if it is possible, let this cup pass from Me. Yet not as I will, but as You will." Instead of refusing the cup of suffering and judgment, Messiah Jesus yielded Himself to Father God's plan. If there had been some other way for humanity to be saved from sin, Jesus would have welcomed it. But there wasn't.

What about you, beloved? When you come to those difficult moments in life when you know you're being challenged by the Word of God and the Holy Spirit to say no to yourself and yes to God, do you try to find a way around it? When you know doing the right thing is going to cause you pain, do you rationalize doing things your own way? Or do you get on your face as Yeshua did and pray, "Not my will but Your will be done"?

This is the heart of a true disciple. It's why Jesus said, "If anyone wishes to come after Me, he must deny himself, and take up his cross and follow Me" (Matt. 16:24). The cross represents dying to self and doing the Father's will.

Some years ago I recognized that I had not been willing to let God be the Lord over what I ate. I love sweets, cookies, candy, and pastries. It was an area in my life that I had not let Jesus in to reign over. I actually subconsciously was saying to Him, "Don't touch that part of my life."

But eventually I learned to say to Him, "Not my will, but Thy will be done" regarding my food choices. As a result, I lost forty pounds, and Yeshua is reigning in and through me in a greater way. Beloved, if the Father has been talking with you about something and you've been unwilling to yield your will to His will, say yes to Him. Tell Him, "Not my will but Your will be done."

We want to come to a place in our lives where the will of God has taken up primary residence in our hearts so we aren't fighting with God all the time about who we are going to obey, ourselves or Him. Every part of our hearts should be bowed to the Father. We must submit every area of our lives to the Father, just as Messiah Yeshua did. Even though it was painful for Him to go to the cross, He bowed Himself in obedience, denied Himself, and said yes to the Father's will.

Will you do the same? Will you choose to walk in obedience? Will you refuse to give in to your flesh and yield to Father God as Jesus did? As you go before Father God in prayer, will you tell Him, "Your wine goes down smoothly; not my will but Your will be done"? (See Song of Solomon 7:9.)

If you choose to surrender your life completely to the Lord, including the areas you've been unwilling to release to Him—if you say yes to God and no to yourself—you're going to operate in greater power and see more of your prayers being answered because you will decrease and Jesus will increase and be magnified in your life (John 3:30).

Faith Over Fear

Even on the cross Yeshua was fully surrendered to the Father. How do we know this? When Jesus was being crucified and His spirit was just about to leave His body, the last thing He said is, "Father, into Your hands I commit My spirit," and after He said this, "He breathed His last" (Luke 23:46).

As a side note, psychiatrists and psychologists tell us that subconsciously mankind's greatest fear is the fear of death. Satan exploits this, using this fear to hold people in bondage their whole lives. The fear of death is the mother of all fears, but many people don't realize they're struggling with this. They have other fears that they are conscious of, but sometimes the root fear, even if they're not aware of it, is the fear of death.

Even when the fear of death is suppressed, it springs forth in various forms. It's like an invisible seed that can sprout up out of your life in strange ways. Maybe you're afraid that when you're driving you're going to lose control of the vehicle and go off the road. Or maybe you have a fear of blurting out something you don't want to say. Or maybe you have a fear of growing old, or of spiders, or of losing a job or going broke. Unconsciously, these fears may ultimately be rooted in the fear of death. In other words, if we are afraid to die because we are afraid of the unknown or of going to hell, even when we are not consciously thinking of dying, other fears can manifest that would not arise if we weren't afraid of dying. It's like having a sore throat due to acid reflux. Your throat hurts, but your real problem is not your throat but the acid from your stomach that is coming up and burning it.

The good news is that we can conquer the fear of death by knowing that when we die we're going to be with God, and once we break the fear of death, we're going to see many of the other fears we have go away. Again, the fear of death represents, ultimately, a fear of the unknown. After all, the greatest unknown is death itself. But Yeshua said, "Into Your hands I commit My spirit." Messiah faced death with confidence because He knew where He was going.

The Bible says Jesus knew that "He had come forth from God and was going back to God" (John 13:3). If you and I don't have confidence that we're going to be with God when we die, we're going to have the ultimate fear of the unknown lurking deep inside us. It's a scary thing when you don't know what you're going to face.

Not knowing where we're going when we die also represents a fear of losing control, which is a tremendous fear. Think about it. When we don't have confidence that we're going to go to and be with God when we die and leave this world, we're going to feel completely out of control. I love what David said in Psalm 17:15, "As for me, I shall behold Your face in righteousness; I will be satisfied with Your likeness when I awake." David had confidence that when he died he would see God. By having a faith rooted in Yeshua the Messiah, we can overcome our fears.

Jesus, deep in His heart, had a tremendous assurance and knowing that when He left this world, He was going to go be with His Father, God, and I want you to have that same confidence. The apostle John wrote, "These things I have written to you who believe in the name of the Son of God, so that you may know that you have eternal life" (1 John 5:13). God wants us to have inner security, as Jesus did, that when we leave this world, we're going to be with Him.

Beloved, I challenge you to believe God's Word. If you have received Jesus into your heart as Messiah, repented of your sins, and turned your life over to the Father, then you can know that when you die you're going to heaven. If you struggle to accept this, ask God to strengthen your faith in His Word so you'll know beyond a shadow of a doubt that you're going to heaven when you die. Ask Him to give you the assurance Jesus had so you too can pray, "Father, into Your hands I commit My spirit." There is no reason to doubt. If you believe in and have turned your life over to the Son of God to truly be the Lord of your life, know you have eternal life.

Father God wants to release assurance over our hearts that we truly belong to Him, that our salvation has been purchased by the blood of Yeshua, and that when we die, we're going to be with Him in heaven.

As you read these words, I break the fear of death off your life with the two-edged sword of God's Word. I loose a wave of the knowledge of God's compassion and love for you. Father, I release an assurance of salvation, in the name of Yeshua HaMashiach, into the hearts of Your people.

Beloved, let's trust Him with our lives, to the point that we say, "Not my will, Lord, but Yours be done. Into Your hands I commit my spirit." He will never leave or forsake us.

Chapter 19

THE FATHER HEARS YOU

Then Jesus raised His eyes, and said, "Father, I thank
You that You have heard Me. I knew that You always
hear Me; but because of the people standing around I
said it, so that they may believe that You sent Me."
—JOHN 11:41–42

JOHN 11:41–42 HAS always been one of my favorite passages of Scripture. Jesus is about to raise Lazarus from the
dead, and He lifts His eyes to heaven, opens His mouth,
and begins to speak loudly enough for all the people around
Him to hear. And this is what He says: "Father, I thank You
that You have heard Me. I knew that You always hear Me; but
because of the people standing around I said it, so that they
may believe that You sent Me." In other words, Jesus was saying,
"Father God, I'm praying out loud so that all the people around
Me know that You hear Me. *I* know You always hear Me; I'm
speaking with My voice so that *they* know You hear Me."

There's something foundational about praying out loud.

There is power in believing God's Word in our hearts and then speaking it out of our mouths. This kind of prayer is dynamic and fundamental to walking with God. When we pray out loud, we are not only verbalizing our faith but we are also using our mouths and vocal cords to stand in agreement with God. But there is another side to praying out loud, and that is knowing that God also hears even the subtlest whisper of our hearts. He knows every thought of our minds. That's what Jesus was saying through this prayer—that the only reason He was praying out loud in that moment was so those around Him would know what He already realized, which is that Father God hears Him, whether He opens His mouth to speak or not.

I want you to understand that God is closer to you than your own breath. He hears you always. God is not way up there in the heavens. You don't have to scream to get His attention. God hears the subtlest movement of your heart. He hears the faintest cry of your soul. He knows every thought in your mind because He's closer to you than you are to yourself.

Father wants us to gain this assurance—that He's not a far-away God we can reach only by shouting to Him. Rather, He's closer to us than our own heartbeat. The apostle Paul tells us that the word of faith "is near you, in your mouth and in your heart" (Rom. 10:8). It is not so far away that we can't reach it. Neither is God so far removed that we can't find Him. His Word is in our mouths and in our hearts.

God wants us to know how intimately acquainted with us He is, that He is in every breath we take. He's in every beat of our hearts. God wants us to realize that He's inside us and we belong to Him. In Yeshua, we're in God and God is in us. The Word tells us "in Him we live and move and have our being"

(Acts 17:28, MEV). Jesus wants us to know He is near to us. He wants us to realize that wherever we go, He is there.

If we think about the future and are afraid, it's because we're imagining a future without God in it. Sometimes we imagine a circumstance that produces anxiety, but if we really consider the thoughts we are having about the future that are causing us distress, we'll realize that God is not in the thoughts we are having. The truth is that wherever we go, God will be there. "He Himself has said, 'I will never desert you, nor will I ever forsake you'" (Heb. 13:5). God will always be in our future. When we experience fear because of a thought about the future, it's because an awareness of God's presence is not in our thought projection. "So do not worry about tomorrow; for tomorrow will care for itself. Each day has enough trouble of its own" (Matt. 6:34).

I heard a story about a girl who was living in anxiety for many months over her fear of getting fired from her job. After months of living in this torment, her boss called her into his office one day and fired her. Her testimony is that when she actually got fired, she wasn't afraid. Why? Because God was with her when it actually happened.

In our fearful future thought projections, we don't sense God. Why? Because God is the God of the present, the God of the now, not the God of vain imaginations that don't in reality exist. Jesus said, "I am in the Father and the Father is in Me" (John 14:11). That's how close Messiah Jesus was to the Father when He walked this earth, and that's how close Father God is to us today. He is so close to us, it's beyond words. It's hard to describe something that is closer to us than our own heartbeat, but that is how close Father God is to us. Scripture says nothing can separate us from the love of God—"neither death, nor life, nor angels, nor principalities, nor things present, nor things to come, nor powers, nor height, nor depth, nor any other created thing" (Rom. 8:38–39). He is with us always, "even to the end of the age" (Matt. 20:28).

Pour Out Your Heart to Him

If we truly understood how present Father God is to us, we would pray as Yeshua prayed. We would be bold and confident before the Lord, knowing that He hears us. We would know that He loves us, cares about us, and wants to respond to us. We would realize that He hears even the faintest whisper of our hearts and responds to us in love, compassion, understanding, and mercy.

In John 12:28, Jesus, speaking of His coming death, said, "'Father, glorify Your name.' Then a voice came out of heaven: 'I have both glorified it, and will glorify it again.'" Notice that after Yeshua spoke to His Father, His Father responded instantly, saying, "I have both glorified it, and will glorify it again." I want you to know that when you open your heart to the Father, He speaks back to you. The problem often is that you and I don't always have ears to hear what He's saying to us, and we can't always perceive His word to us because His ways are higher than our ways, even as the heavens are higher than the earth (Isa. 55:8–9). But when you and I are crying out to God, He's responding to us. When we pray to God in earnestness and faith, and in a way that's pleasing to Him, He is going to respond.

Sometimes if we don't receive an answer to our prayers right away or don't see God move immediately, we think He's not responding or doesn't hear. But we must remember that "with the Lord one day is like a thousand years, and a thousand years like one day" (2 Pet. 3:8). I once heard a man give a great illustration of this. He said imagine someone being way up high in a hot-air balloon, watching a parade. All the parade is going by below: first the trumpet blowers, then the floats for local businesses, then the mayor's float, then the kids' floats.

The people watching from the street see each part of the processional one float at a time, and it takes about twenty minutes for the whole parade to go by. But the person in the hot air balloon doesn't see each individual phase of the parade. As the person looks down on it from way up in the sky, he sees the whole parade at once.

God's perspective of time is different from ours. His is like the person's in the hot air balloon, who sees everything at once rather than seeing the floats one by one over a length of time like the people standing along the street. He sees the end from the beginning (Isa. 46:10), and even when we don't know what Father God is doing, we should be confident that He is answering the cry of our hearts.

As you know, prayer is not one-sided, where we just talk to God as some type of therapy to get something off our chest. No, prayer is living and dynamic, and the Father is responding to His kids.

Notice also that in John 12:27, before going to the cross, Jesus said, "Now My soul has become troubled." I want to point out that Messiah Yeshua was talking to the Father about His feelings. He was sharing His life with the Father. You may have thought, "The Lord knows everything about me, so why should I have to tell Him about myself?" God wants us to share our lives with Him. Our Creator wants us to talk to Him. He wants to be in relationship with you and me, and He wants us to experience Him subjectively.

There is a difference between the Father knowing something objectively and us inviting Him in to experience our lives with us. There's a difference between Him knowing everything about us and us talking to Him as a friend about what's going on so He can participate in our lives. Jesus wants to dwell inside us. Yeshua said, "Behold, I stand at the door and knock; if anyone hears My voice and opens the door, I will come in to him and will dine with him, and he with Me" (Rev. 3:20). This happens primarily as we talk with God.

Even as Messiah told Father that His soul had become troubled, so too the Lord wants us to talk to Him about our lives. Obviously, this dialogue between the Father and Yeshua in John 12:27 was the result of the weight Messiah was about to bear in dying for the sins of the world, which cannot be compared to the weight we bear—we bear only our own struggles; Jesus bore the weight of the sin of the whole world—but the point is still the same. Jesus opened His soul and emotions as He talked to His Father. God wants us to talk to Him about everything. He wants us to share our thoughts and emotions with Him. You may have a best friend whom you tell everything. You know what? God wants you to tell Him first. He wants you to talk to Him more than you talk with your best friend. The apostle John felt so close to Jesus he leaned his head on Yeshua's bosom (John 13:23). Yeshua wants us to feel the same way.

Talk to God, beloved. Share your life with Him. I hear the Father calling you His kid, speaking to you individually as His child, and saying, "Talk to Me." He wants you to know Him as your papa. God is holy and worthy of our honor and respect, but He doesn't want you to think He's distant and untouchable.

He wants to nurture, comfort, and guide you. Let's open our hearts and let Him in.

You don't have to be afraid to tell God anything. Tell Him what angers you. Tell Him all about yourself. He knows already, but when you talk to Him, you're going to build intimacy with Him, and He's going to be pleased that you've opened your heart to Him. Read the Psalms. David was totally open and honest with God.

If you have a wrong attitude, the way to get cleansed and healed is to talk to Him about it. If you're unsure of what step to take in life, the answer is to talk with God about it. If you need healing in a relationship, pour your heart out to the Lord. As you do, the Spirit of God is going to move deeper into your heart and gain greater possession of you. His Spirit will run more and more fully through you as you open up to Him.

Beloved, God hears you—whether you speak in a shout or a whisper, whether you pray out loud or silently—and He's responding to you. Talk to Him. Have faith that He loves you. I believe the Father is saying to you right now: "My child, be encouraged. I love you. Keep talking to Me. Keep praying to Me. Keep opening your heart to Me. I want to intimately be involved in your life. Walk with Me; I am walking with you."

Trust Him, dear one. Even when you can't see what is happening, Father God is moving on your behalf.

Chapter 20

JESUS' HIGH PRIESTLY PRAYER

> Jesus spoke these things; and lifting up His eyes to heaven,
> He said, "Father, the hour has come; glorify Your Son,
> that the Son may glorify You, even as You gave Him
> authority over all flesh, that to all whom You have given
> Him, He may give eternal life. This is eternal life, that
> they may know You, the only true God, and Jesus Christ
> whom You have sent....That they may be one, just as We
> are one...so that the world may know that You sent Me."
> —JOHN 17:1–3, 22–23

BEFORE JESUS WENT to the cross, He interceded for us, praying what is often called the high priestly prayer. In the Old Testament, the high priest went before the Lord to make sacrifices to atone for the sin of the people and intercede for them. This is what Yeshua did in John 17 as He was preparing to become the ultimate sacrifice for our sins on the cross. He went before the Father and prayed not only for Himself and His disciples but also for you and me.

Through this prayer, the longest prayer of Yeshua's recorded in the Gospels, we see the inner dimension of Messiah's heart and the way God's kingdom operates in and upon us through the Holy Spirit. Again, through Yeshua's prayer for us we gain a better understanding of exactly who He is and what He desires for each of us. And when we pray as Yeshua prayed with a sincere heart, we know God will answer. So in this chapter we will look at key verses from the high priestly prayer to understand what we too should be seeking from and asking of the Father.

To Glorify God

Jesus began His prayer in John 17 by lifting His eyes to heaven and saying, "Father, the hour has come; glorify Your Son, that the Son may glorify You" (v. 1). Even as Father glorified Yeshua, so too your destiny is for Jesus to be exalted through your life so the Father will be glorified. God's purpose is that you would be like a city on a hill that everybody can see. It's that you would be a sign and a wonder and people would see the supernatural nature of God through your life and as a result look to the Father and give Him glory.

So ask God to glorify Himself through your life. Don't just beat yourself up and say you're a worthless sinner. No, you're a sinner who has been forgiven by the grace of God, and God's purpose is to glorify Jesus through your life. The Scripture says, "For those whom He foreknew, He also predestined to become conformed to the image of His Son, so that He would be the firstborn among many brethren; and these whom He predestined, He also called; and these whom He called, He also justified; and these whom He justified, He also glorified" (Rom. 8:29–30).

I think oftentimes throughout our history, we as believers

have heard a gospel preached that only makes us sin-conscious. For so many years we sang songs with lyrics like "Amazing grace, how sweet the sound that saved a wretch like me," which made us think of ourselves primarily as sinners who had been forgiven. We didn't have a paradigm to understand that yes, we are sinners saved by grace, but the Lord no longer wants us to primarily identify with our sinfulness but with the fact that we are new creations in Yeshua.

Our Creator wants us to look beyond where we've been and where we are to see where we're going—a place where we allow the Lord to glorify Himself through our lives. So let's pray as Jesus did. Yeshua asked the Father to glorify Him so God would be glorified through His life. Let's ask Father God to do the same thing through us.

To Know Him

Yeshua continued in John 17:2, "Even as You gave Him authority over all flesh, that to all whom You have given Him, He may give eternal life." Jesus understood that His mission was to give eternal life to those whom the Father had given Him. This is what Messiah Jesus was speaking of in John 6 when He said:

> This is the will of Him who sent Me, that of all that He has given Me I lose nothing, but raise it up on the last day.
> —JOHN 6:39

> No one can come to Me unless the Father who sent Me draws him; and I will raise him up on the last day.
> —JOHN 6:44

> For this reason I have said to you, that no one can come to
> Me unless it has been granted him from the Father.
>
> —John 6:65

Then, after making the point that He came to bring eternal life to all whom the Father had given Him, Jesus said in verse 3, "This is eternal life, that they may know You, the only true God, and Jesus Christ whom You have sent." We see into the mystery of what eternity is all about as we look at Jesus' words in this verse. Messiah defines *eternal life* as *knowing God*. You see, salvation is all about relationship. Going to heaven is about being in relationship with God. Everyone who believes receives eternal life, and eternal life is the gift of knowing God.

So praying as Jesus prayed involves asking Father God to bring us more and more fully into the dimension of really experientially knowing Him. We don't want to have a form of religion, where we know certain precepts, teachings, and doctrines and just have a bunch of intellectual information in our heads. We want to know Him. This is the only truth there is—knowing Father God. Before He went to the cross, Jesus prayed that we would have eternal life, and He told us that eternal life was to know Him and the Father.

To Accomplish His Work

Yeshua continued by telling the Father, "I glorified You on the earth, having accomplished the work which You have given Me to do" (v. 4). Messiah Jesus is pouring out His love to the Father in John 17, and it is clear in this verse that Yeshua does not separate loving God from working for God. Jesus came to earth because of His love for the Father. He accomplished the work our Creator gave Him to do. This means that if we love God, we have to do the work He gives us to do.

Some years ago my wife, Cynthia, and I went out fishing with a guide in Colorado. It had been our first time fly-fishing together. We had to travel over an hour in our guide's car to get to the spot where we were going to fish, and once we arrived it was such a beautiful experience. Whether it was the beauty of nature that enthralled us or the fact we were catching fish, we had a great day.

Then, on the way home, as we were traveling with our guide back to the fly-fishing shop, I knew I had to share the good news of Messiah Jesus and the kingdom of heaven with him. It was hard to bring the subject up because we had been getting along so well and I knew that challenging him with the good news of Yeshua could potentially break our friendship and connection. But I feel a mandate from the Father to be His light and ambassador in the earth and to preach and declare the good news of Jesus wherever I am. So I brought up the subject and talked to him about the love of God and Jesus being the only way into a relationship with the Creator.

Just as I was concerned might happen, he was offended and it did break that sense of connection we had felt all day together. I tried to move the relationship forward, but the conversation wasn't quite the same, and eventually he dropped us off at the fly-fishing shop. Later that evening, Cynthia and I went out to eat. As we sat at a table outside to enjoy the beautiful evening, she brought up how easy it is for me to witness to people as she recalled the episode she had observed when I shared the gospel with our guide.

When she said it was so easy for me, I literally started crying because so often it is the opposite of easy. It's hard. It hurts. It's painful to be rejected because of my witness for the kingdom of heaven. I explained to Cynthia that it's not easy; it's painful, but this is the work God has given me to do. We are His witnesses.

Before Jesus went to the cross, He was sweating blood and said, "Father, if it is possible, let this cup pass from Me." But then He said, "This is the reason I came into the world." We must finish the work God has given us to do. It may not be enjoyable or easy, but like Yeshua we must do the work the Father has given us to do.

Jesus said later in John 17, "As You sent Me into the world, I also have sent them into the world" (v. 18). What are we sent to do? We're sent to preach the gospel, lay our hands on and pray for the sick, and take authority over the powers of darkness in people's lives. We're called to extend the territory of the kingdom. Everywhere Yeshua went, He did three things: He preached the gospel, healed the sick, and drove out demons. Matthew 4:23–24 says, "Jesus was going throughout all Galilee, teaching in their synagogues and proclaiming the gospel of the kingdom, and healing every kind of disease and every kind of sickness among the people. The news about Him spread throughout all Syria; and they brought to Him all who were ill, those suffering with various diseases and pains, demoniacs, epileptics, paralytics; and He healed them."

Yeshua instructs us to carry on this same work. He said in Matthew 10, "And as you go, preach, saying, 'The kingdom of heaven is at hand.' Heal the sick, raise the dead, cleanse the lepers, cast out demons. Freely you received, freely give" (vv. 7–8). Even as Messiah Jesus loved God by accomplishing the work the Father gave Him to do, so too do we need to show our love for our Creator by working for Him while on earth.

This is what He was calling Peter to do when He asked him, "Do you love Me?" When Peter replied, "Lord, You know I love You," Yeshua told him, "Feed My sheep. Show your love for Me by doing the work of the Father." (See John 21:17.)

We can't separate loving God from working for Him. We can't just sit in our homes all the time listening to teaching CDs, watching Christian television, and listening to worship music. We must get out, help people, and spread the gospel if we're healthy enough to do so. If we love God, we must do as Jesus instructed Peter and go take care of His people.

So let's ask Father God to help us kick our love factor to the next level by activating us to do the work He has called us to do. Let's become greater servants. Let's build the kingdom. Let's witness more. Let's love more. Let's care for people more. Let's take care of the elderly. Let's help those who are sick. Let's share the gospel with our neighbors. Let's invite people over for a meal. Let's help the poor. Let's be movers and shakers for the kingdom of God. We must love the Lord by doing His work.

To Receive Supernatural Protection

In verse 11 of His prayer Messiah said, "I am no longer in the world; and yet they themselves are in the world, and I come to You. Holy Father, keep them in Your name, the name which You have given Me." I want you to understand that the Father is keeping you and there's a supernatural hedge of protection around your life.

The Bible tells us in Psalm 91, "He who dwells in the shelter of the Most High will abide in the shadow of the Almighty. I will say to the LORD, 'My refuge and my fortress, my God, in whom I trust!'...A thousand may fall at your side and ten thousand at your right hand, but it shall not approach you" (vv. 1, 3, 7). Then the Lord says, "Because he has loved Me, therefore I will deliver him....He will call upon Me, and I will answer him; I will be with him in trouble; I will rescue him and honor him" (Ps. 91:14–16).

God is your refuge, and He wants you to feel safe and secure in Him. Even if something happens that looks tragic from the world's perspective, when you go through it, you're going to be protected in God, just as Stephen was in the Book of Acts when he was being stoned to death. As I already shared in an earlier chapter, from the outside it looked like Stephen was suffering one of the most violent deaths in the world. Yet while he was being hit with all those stones, Stephen, full of the Holy Spirit, "gazed intently into heaven and saw the glory of God, and Jesus standing at the right hand of God; and he said, 'Behold, I see the heavens opened up and the Son of Man standing at the right hand of God'" (Acts 7:55–56).

From the outside it looked like Stephen wasn't protected, but in reality he was. And that same supernatural protection is around your life. Jesus prayed for it in John 17:11 when He said, "Father, keep them in Your name." My friend, you don't have to wonder or worry whether God will guard you. You can have complete confidence that you are protected in the *shalom* and love of God.

In verse 12 Jesus continued this same theme and said, "While I was with them, I was keeping them in Your name which You have given Me; and I guarded them and not one of them perished but the son of perdition, so that the Scripture would be fulfilled." I want you to know that if not one perished when Messiah Jesus guarded them on earth, you can also trust that you are being guarded all the days of your life. That doesn't mean you and I will never go through anything tragic; many of the apostles lost their lives because of their testimony. It means that in the midst of everything, we're guarded and the grace of God in our lives is our greatest reality and victory.

You're protected, my beloved friend. Be secure in that. When you pray for God's protection on your life, you can be sure that He will answer. Although the world lies in the power of the evil one (John 5:19), you are being guarded by your Creator and your life has a supernatural protective barrier around it. Jesus prayed, "I do not ask You to take them out of the world, but to keep them from the evil one" (John 17:15).

To Have His Joy

In verse 13 Jesus said to the Father, "But now I come to You...so that they may have *My joy made full in themselves*" (emphasis added). Everybody wants to be happy. Jesus prayed for our happiness because His will is for us to be happy on the inside.

Yeshua said that the joy and peace He gives us are not from the world. The joy and peace the world gives are rooted in circumstance; they're rooted to something that's outside ourselves. In other words, we get a new house and we're happy. We get a new car and we're happy. We go on vacation and we're happy. We succeed at something and we're happy. Those sources of happiness are all rooted in externals, and the problem with external forms of peace and happiness is that they are temporary. They can never last because the circumstances always change.

I thank God for all the blessings He gives us in our circumstances. But there's something deeper, something more, and it's the joy and the peace that come from the internal working and operation of the Holy Spirit in our hearts. The joy Messiah Jesus gives is not of the world.

Consider this. Yeshua's first miracle in the Gospel of John was when He turned water into wine. Have you ever wondered why? Wine in Scripture is a symbol of earthly celebration. It's served during times of great joy. I find that interesting. Yeshua's first miracle was at a place where the focus was on celebration and joy. People were watching their loved ones get married. They were happy and having a great time. Yet it's hard for many of us to believe God wants us to be happy. Some of us have been so beaten down by preaching on the consequences of sin and judgment that we see God as more angry than happy. But Jesus prayed that our joy would be made full. Beloved, God is happy; it's an essential part of His nature.

One of the most famous sermons in Christian history is called "Sinners in the Hands of an Angry God." It was preached hundreds of years ago by an eighteenth-century revivalist named Jonathan Edwards, and we still hear this type of message going forth. That sermon brought great revival during the 1700s, but at the end of the day, if the only thing that's motivating us to serve Jesus is a fear of punishment and judgment, our joy will never be made full.

Scripture says the fear of God is the beginning of wisdom (Prov. 9:10). But there's something greater, and that's the revelation of the love of God. When we have a revelation of the love of God in addition to a revelation of the fear of God, we're going to have joy. When we realize how much God loves us and how special we are to Him, we'll have true joy. When we have confidence that the future is going to be good because Jesus is always going to be with us in our tomorrows, we'll understand and experience the type of joy Yeshua was asking the Father for on our behalf.

God wants you to have joy, not predominantly from the things of the world but in and through Him. Begin to participate in this by activating your will to come into alignment with this truth. Confess when you go to bed at night: "Father God, today was a good day, and tomorrow is going to be a good day because You're going to be with me tomorrow. Goodness and lovingkindness are going to follow me all the days of my life, according to Psalm 23. Thank You that You're using everything that I go through in life every day to bring me closer to You!"

Again, our Father wants us to be confident in His future for us. He wants us to be secure in the fact that our future is going to be good and bright. The Book of Ephesians tells us in chapters 1 and 2 that God saved us in order that He might show His kindness and goodness toward us for the rest of eternity. In other words, Father saved you so He could keep showing you His kindness and goodness forever and ever. Grabbing hold of this truth will make you happy. Scripture says, "But God, being rich in mercy, because of His great love with which He loved us, even when we were dead in our transgressions, made us alive together with Christ (by grace you have been saved)...so that in the ages to come He might show the surpassing riches of His grace in kindness toward us in Christ Jesus" (Eph. 2:4–5, 7).

If you've been operating under a spirit of gloom and doom; if you grew up in a home of sadness, melancholy, and depression; if your personality is flat and you can never get excited about anything, I want you to know, your Creator has something better for you. Jesus said, "I came that they may have life, and have it abundantly" (John 10:10). Say *yes* to joy. Cast off spirits of depression, loneliness, and isolation, spirits of gloom and doom and rejection. Tear down every demonic stronghold of darkness and declare that the oil of gladness is on you to displace the spirit of heaviness according to Isaiah 61:3.

We serve a happy God, not a sad God, and He's in us and we're in Him. So from this point on, declare that you're going to move forward in joy, that you're going to practice having a spirit of celebration and thankfulness. Thanking Father and Jesus for who They are and all They have done in your life will move you into joy.

It glorifies Messiah Yeshua when His people live with a spirit of joy, because people see that joy in us, and when we tell them it's because of Jesus, Yeshua becomes attractive to them. Jesus wants His fragrance to shine through us, and part of this involves walking as a people of confidence and joy. Again, God wants you to be happy, not because of what the world can give, but because of Him. Believe it. Declare it. Step into it. War for it if you have to, but make up your mind that you're going to be happy and full of joy because you're a child of God.

To Receive God's Word

Next, in verse 14, Jesus said, "I have given them Your word." Receiving God's Word is the way to become strong and happy. Yeshua said in John 6:63, "The words that I have spoken to you are spirit and are life." And He said in John 6:35, "I am the bread of life; he who comes to Me will not hunger, and he who believes in Me will never thirst."

Jesus went on to say in John 6:53–58, "Truly, truly, I say to you, unless you eat the flesh of the Son of Man and drink His blood, you have no life in yourselves. He who eats My flesh and drinks My blood has eternal life, and I will raise him up on the last day. For My flesh is true food, and My blood is true drink. He who eats My flesh and drinks My blood abides in Me, and I in him. As the living Father sent Me, and I live because of the Father, so he who eats Me, he also will live because of Me. This is the bread which came down out of heaven; not as the fathers ate and died; he who eats this bread will live forever."

The Word of God is living and active (Heb. 4:12). It is spirit and life (John 6:63). It is what we live by. Declare that out loud. Say, "I've made up my mind by the Spirit of Jesus to seize God's Word, as Yeshua does, and not let anything else in." Messiah said, "I have given them Your Word." So say out loud again, "Lord God, I seize Your Word. I receive it and will not let anything else in."

Then He prayed in verse 17, "Sanctify them in the truth; Your word is truth." Sanctification is a type of washing. So Yeshua prayed that we would be washed of all defilement and sanctified in His truth and Word, which are the only true reality.

Then Jesus continued in verse 18, "As You sent Me into the world, I also have sent them into the world." As I said previously, we can't separate our love for God from doing the work of God. We need to be His witnesses. We need to share His Word. We need to tell the world that we love Him. We need to tell our friends, neighbors, and work associates that Jesus is alive, speaks to us, and answers our prayers, and that He is real. Some of us should start Bible studies in our homes. If you are one the Lord is speaking to about starting a Bible study in your home, know that you don't need to be an expert Bible teacher. Just start. (One easy way to do this is to simply record or purchase the DVDs to my teachings, listen to them together, and then use the notes for each teaching, which are free online at discoveringthejewishjesus.com. This is just one option; there are many good resources out there.)

We, God's church, have been sent into the world to preach the gospel to all creation and make disciples of all nations. Some of us have been given five talents, another two, and another one. Do you remember this parable that Jesus told in Matthew 25:14–30? Not all of us are in the same physical condition, nor do we all have the same abilities or have access to the same number of people. But the important thing is for us to do what we can when we can for the kingdom of God, to be His witnesses and light in the earth.

To Be One

Jesus continued in verse 21, "That they may all be one; even as You, Father, are in Me and I in You, that they also may be in Us, so that the world may believe that You sent Me." Jesus is praying for the unity of His body, the church, that we would walk in oneness. Paul called for this same thing in Ephesians 4, "With all humility and gentleness, with patience, showing tolerance for one another in love, being diligent to preserve the unity of the Spirit in the bond of peace. There is one body and one Spirit, just as also you were called in one hope of your calling" (vv. 2–4). I've seen a lot of people start attending a congregation somewhere, and as soon as they have a disagreement with the pastor, the rabbi, or somebody in the congregation, they leave. But you know what? No one and nowhere is perfect. We're never going to grow if we run from a relationship every time we have a conflict.

I have grown so much in my life from working through problems in relationships. The Father has built so much maturity into me as I have learned to accept my responsibility when any division in a relationship is a result of my immaturity, my wrong perception about the situation, or some type of sin in my heart. I also have discovered more effective ways of communicating with someone I'm having a conflict with. For example, saying, "You did this, and it made me mad," just makes a person defensive. But if I say, "You know, it hurt me when you did this," the person is able to hear what I have to say, and then we can dialogue about it. We can work through it together rather than running from it.

God's Spirit wants there to be oneness among His people, but too many of us immediately close the door when we have a problem in a relationship and block the person from our lives. Sometimes that's the right thing to do, but usually the right thing to do is to continue to love and try to find a way through the breach in the relationship. And one of the primary ways we can get past difficult situations in relationships—and there will always be difficulties in any relationship—is through communicating rather than separating ourselves.

Let's commit to working through things instead of going from church to church, spouse to spouse, or job to job, so we can grow in maturity and love. Let's be willing to walk through our difficulties. Let's talk the problem through without blame and anger as much as possible, looking for a way to resolve the situation, grow together, and stay unified, because this shows maturity in our lives and in the body of Christ. This is what Jesus prayed for. He said that when His people are unified, God's kingdom shines into the earth. "By this all men will know that you are My disciples, if you have love for one another" (John 13:35).

The unity of the Spirit through His church needs to be reflected in the home and family unit as well. I've been married for more than thirty years now, and it is all by the grace of God. My wife and I have worked together all these years to become one. We've worked through things. We've prayed together. We've talked together. It's been a struggle, but through it all, a unity has been developed over time, a unity of the Spirit. It's a beautiful thing. This is what God wants to develop in your life. He wants the world to see unity in the church and in our relationships.

To Participate in His Glory

After praying for our unity, Yeshua told the Father that He has given us, the church, the glory that the Father has given Him "that they may be one, just as We are one" (v. 22). Beloved, we are called to participate in His glory. He wants us to be partakers of it. We are destined for it. Scripture says, "And these whom He predestined, He also called; and these whom He called, He also justified; and these whom He justified, He also glorified" (Rom. 8:30). Let me tell you, that is something worth living for.

The Hebrew word for *glory* is *kavod*, and it speaks of a weightiness of God's presence. When Jesus is speaking of God's glory, He's speaking of the weight of God's presence. He's speaking of the fact that God is in the process of immersing His church— washing us and imparting into us—His presence. I want you to know that eye has not seen and ear has not heard the things that are awaiting you in God's kingdom. And the good news is that you and I can keep entering in to more and more of it.

We are on a journey of discovery. Yeshua said, "If you continue in My word, then you are truly disciples of Mine" (John 8:31). Notice Jesus said we must continue in His Word. We are in a process of progressive revelation, meaning that Messiah intends for us to keep asking, keep seeking, and keep knocking so we will enter more and more into an experiential reality of the glory of God in and on our lives.

Once again, Jesus said in verse 22, "The glory which You have given Me I have given to them." But just as the Israelites were given the physical land of Israel yet had to drive out the Amorites, Hittites, Jebusites, and others to take possession of it, you and I also have to press in to enter the fullness of what our Creator has given us. Father God has given us His glory, but we must seek it, ask for it, knock, and obey. As we do, we're going to find ourselves encountering the Lord in ever-growing weights of His presence.

Don't let these words fall away like water off a duck's back. Believe that God wants you to encounter Him through His Holy Spirit and His Word. Believe that you can experience Messiah. Yeshua said He has given us His glory. The weight of Father's presence is your portion as God's child.

You may experience seasons of dryness, but life is a series of battles and then increased releases in God's joy and glory. By that I mean we go through battles, we go through trials, and then when we get through that season of battling and trial, the Lord releases us into a new dimension of joy and glory. Because Christ was formed in us in a deeper way by going through the trial, Scripture says that as we walk with God through our trials an "eternal weight of glory" is being formed in us. In other words, God establishes us in Himself as we rely on and cling to Him through times of dryness or trials.

For momentary, light affliction is producing for us an eternal weight of glory far beyond all comparison.

—2 CORINTHIANS 4:17

Consider it all joy, my brethren, when you encounter various trials, knowing that the testing of your faith produces endurance. And let endurance have its perfect result, so that you may be perfect and complete, lacking in nothing.

—JAMES 1:2–4

So hear me: I am not saying that growing and experiencing God's glory involves no suffering. No, we have to go through many trials and overcome many challenges in life. Life on this side of heaven involves both joy and suffering. Paul said that we suffer with Jesus in order to be glorified with Him: "And if children, heirs also, heirs of God and fellow heirs with Christ, if indeed we suffer with Him so that we may also be glorified with Him" (Rom. 8:17). And Luke said, "Through many tribulations we must enter the kingdom of God" (Acts 14:22). Yes, there is suffering and pain on the earth right now, but in the midst of it we experience God's glory! The Creator Himself is with you, and you have overcome the world in Him. (See 1 John 5:4.)

So let's keep pressing on. Let's keep overcoming! Messiah said seven times in Revelation chapters 2 and 3, "He that overcomes will inherit these things and be with Me in the paradise of God." (See Revelation 2:7, 2:11, 2:17, 2:26, 3:5, 3:12, and 3:21.) We've been called to glory, but we must want it, we must seek it, we must ask for it, and we must be faithful to God by loving Him first.

To Be With Him

Yeshua enters into the climax of His prayer in verse 23, praying that we would encounter His incredible love. Jesus is asking the Father to cause us and the world to know He loves us even as He loves Jesus. Do you realize what that means? It means Father God loves you and me with the same strength and in the same way that He loves Yeshua Himself.

Oh that you and I would get a deeper revelation of this truth and know the height and depth and breadth and width of the love of God that is ours in Christ Jesus (Rom. 8:37–39). Our Creator Himself loves you with the same love with which He loves Yeshua.

Next, Messiah Yeshua prayed that we would be with Him in heaven. Why? Because He *wants* to be with us. He gets enjoyment out of being with you and me. He said: "Father, I desire that they also, whom You have given Me, *be with Me where I am*, so that they may see My glory which You have given Me, for You loved Me before the foundation of the world" (v. 24). Isn't this incredible? Those of us who belong to Jesus are going to heaven. Once more, "eye has not seen, nor ear heard, nor has it entered into the heart of man the things which God has prepared for those who love Him" (1 Cor. 2:9, MEV).

Scripture gives us a few scenes of heaven. One that I love is revealed in Isaiah 6 and Revelation 4 when the prophet Isaiah and the apostle John see into heaven. I've talked about this in previous chapters, but the revelation is so rich and meaningful it bears repeating here. In both scenarios, Isaiah and John see God on the throne and all these angels around the throne that don't cease crying out day and night, *kadosh, kadosh, kadosh*—holy, holy, holy is the Lord God Almighty.

Every time they say the word *kadosh*, it's because a new wave, a new revelation, a new impartation, a new manifestation, a new transference of the glory of God comes upon them. Every time they say *holy* it's because they're responding to a new experience and a new dimension of the love and glory of God. Huge ocean waves of God's glory are going to wash over us forevermore. It's going to take our breath away forever and ever as Jesus allows us to be with Him and experience the glory of God, which is alive, everlasting, always changing, and always new.

That's what your God has in store for you. That's why Jesus said He endured the cross and despised the shame for the joy that was set before Him (Heb. 12:2). That's why Paul got to the end of his life and said he had fought a good fight, he had finished the race, and now there was laid up for him the crown of righteousness (2 Tim. 4:7–8). We endure a lot of things in this world, but we must keep our eyes on Lord Yeshua and be faithful because of what is ahead of us. Our permanent home is not here. We're building a habitation in heaven through the things we're doing down here. Jesus is going to reward each one of us according to what we've done (Matt. 16:27), all through His grace!

Our Creator wants us to be with Him where He is so we can behold His glory. Can you imagine? We're going to see the beauty of our Creator, the beauty of the fountain of living waters. David said, "One thing have I desired of the LORD, that will I seek after; that I may dwell in the house of the LORD all the days of my life, to behold the beauty of the LORD" (Ps. 27:4, KJV). In heaven, we're going to see the glory of Jesus. We're going to see the One who is the author of all beauty. We're going to see this One who is everlasting life forever and ever.

Being in heaven is not just seeing Him with our eyes, but literally and fully receiving Him and having Him live through us. I mean, what can we say? Words are inadequate to express what it's going to be like when we're fully participating in a reality that right now we can barely describe with our words. We see through the glass dimly, the Scripture says (1 Cor. 13:12). But this is where we're going. Heaven is our destination, and our time on earth is so short. When we die, we're going to be in God's presence in a snap. "Beloved, now we are children of God, and it has not appeared as yet what we will be. We know that when He appears, we will be like Him, because we will see Him just as He is" (1 John 3:2). This is the wonderful future in store for us in Jesus.

To Receive Revelation of the Father's Love

Yeshua's final words in this prayer are, "I have made Your name known to them"—and I love this—"and will make it known, so that the love with which You loved Me may be in them, and I in them." When Yeshua speaks about revealing the name of God, He's talking about revealing the person of God. He's talking about revealing God Himself to us by His Spirit.

Perhaps best of all, Jesus said, "...and will make it known." This means God is going to *continue* to reveal Himself to you and me. This is why we must keep seeking Him, because God wants to keep revealing Himself. I don't know for sure what fresh part of God's nature, character, or personality Jesus may reveal to me today or tomorrow or next week. But I have faith that Yeshua is going to keep revealing Father to me.

Now receive this: Yeshua prays, "I have made Your name known to them, and will make it known, *so that the love with which You loved Me may be in them, and I in them*" (emphasis added). This means we have been called to have a conscious, experiential reality of knowing the love of God in our lives in the same way Jesus knows the love of the Father in His life.

This is why Messiah Yeshua was saying in essence, "Father, I will keep revealing You to them so that the same love that is in Me may be in them." God is going to keep revealing Himself to you as you seek Him and focus on His Word. And you will receive more and more of the revelation of who Abba is, how much the Father loves you, how protected you are, and your identity and destiny in Him. The same love that's in Jesus is going to be established and ingrained in you. The *kavod* of God—the weight of His presence—will enter you more and more until you will eventually be overcome with the love of God.

We can't fully comprehend how much the Father loves Jesus, but we can imagine a little bit. God's love is all focused on Yeshua, and we're in Yeshua. Messiah is praying that we would understand that the same strength of love that's focused upon Him from the Father is in you and me. And He desires that the love of our Creator would have a home in our hearts, that it would rest on our souls and we would embrace it, move in it, and have our being in it.

The Bible says he who has been perfected in love has no fear (1 John 4:18). The more that you know God loves you, the more at rest you'll be. Your worries will go away. Your fears will go away. Your insecurities will go away. Self-defensiveness will go away. You'll be free in the love of God. This is the destiny

Yeshua is praying for you and me, and if He's praying it, it will surely come to pass.

⚜

Beloved, pray for this. Pray for every word in Yeshua's high priestly prayer to be fully operative and fulfilled in your life. Ask Messiah Jesus to come and have His way in your life. Ask Him to create a resting place for Himself in your heart. As you say yes to Him fully, you will enter into a new realm of knowing God and walking with Him, and the Lord will enter deeper and deeper into you. The more fully you yield to Him, the more He will come in.

Jesus said, "In that day you will know that I am in My Father, and you in Me, and I in you. He who has My commandments and keeps them is the one who loves Me; and he who loves Me will be loved by My Father, and I will love him and will disclose Myself to him....If anyone loves Me, he will keep My word; and My Father will love him, and We will come to him and make Our abode with him" (John 14:20–21, 23). "Behold, I stand at the door and knock; if anyone hears My voice and opens the door, I will come in to him and will dine with him, and he with Me" (Rev. 3:20).

FINAL THOUGHTS

Many of us have been taught to pray audibly, and there is a place for that. But I believe Jesus' prayer life was probably a lot different from many of ours. I believe it was more of an internal conversation with the Father. Why? Because Yeshua walked in the realities we've been reading about in this book. When Yeshua healed people, He didn't stop and say, "Father, will You heal this person?" He knew He had been given healing power, and He just commanded the person to be healed. That's how closely He walked with the Father.

To move into a deeper level of knowing Father God, we must believe that He hears even the slightest impulse of our hearts. Sometimes we think we have to pray out loud for God to hear us, but the Lord wants to bring us to the place where we know He always hears us and we simply live and walk in the reality of that knowing. This will bring us into a deeper place of fellowship with Him, and our perspective will shift from seeing Him as the God who is out "there" somewhere to realizing instead that He is the God who is right here with us and in us. This is why Yeshua said, "The kingdom of God does not come with observation; nor will they say, 'See here!' or 'See there!' For indeed, the kingdom of God is within you" (Luke 17:20–21, NKJV).

To come to this place involves great trust and courage. I know in my own prayer life, it took courage for me to pray out loud less often because I was afraid that if I didn't pray audibly, somehow I would become disconnected from the Lord. This was a scary place to be, but I had to trust that He would take me into a deeper place of knowing Him as I had childlike faith and simply believed.

So as we close this book, I want to encourage you. As you pray the prayers we've outlined in these pages, know that even as you think about the concepts in these prayers, God is partnering and fellowshipping with you, and He's moving you closer and closer to Himself. The Word of God says, "In returning and rest you shall be saved; in quietness and confidence shall be your strength" (Isa. 30:15, NKJV). God is with you, beloved; He's closer even than your own breath. You don't have to shout and scream to be heard. You can have confidence that He always hears you, and He will answer. Just "be still, and know that [He] is God" (Ps. 46:10, NKJV).

NOTES

Chapter 2

1. Sam Walter Foss, "The Prayer of Cyrus Brown," Verse, accessed November 17, 2021, https://verse.press/poem/the-prayer-of-cyrus-brown-27003.

Chapter 8

1. Blue Letter Bible, s.v. "'ēlîyâ," accessed August 16, 2021, https://www.blueletterbible.org/lexicon/h452/kjv/wlc/0-1/.

DISCOVERING THE JEWISH JESUS

CONNECT
WITH RABBI SCHNEIDER

www.DiscoveringTheJewishJesus.com

 /Discovering the Jewish Jesus with Rabbi Schneider

facebook.com/rabbischneider

@RabbiSchneider

Roku—Discovering the Jewish Jesus

 Apple TV—Discovering the Jewish Jesus

amazon Amazon App—Discovering the Jewish Jesus

 Podcast—Discovering the Jewish Jesus

Search for Rabbi Schneider and Discovering the Jewish
Jesus on your favorite platform.